Character Portraits of England's Plantagenet Kings

1132-1485 A.D.

Chris Stubbs

TRAFFORD
Publishing

Trafford rev. 03/06/2013

Trafford
PUBLISHING®   www.trafford.com

North America & international
toll-free: 1 888 232 4444 (USA & Canada)
phone: 250 383 6864 ♦ fax: 812 355 4082

Books written previously by the same author:

'Our Birth on Earth'

'When Scorpio Ruled the World'

'Heaven's Message—How to Read it Nowadays'

ACKNOWLEDGEMENTS

Lois Rodden's website, 'Astro.com' proved invaluable for abstracting much of the rated birth data.

Many thanks must go to the friendly and helpful staff of Wirral Libraries, particularly at the Bromborough branch, who handled unceasing requests for individual biographies for this and previous books with charm and equanimity.

To all those who love the Kings and Queens of England

FOREWORD

"As the king's character went, so went the kingdom."

Just before the Queen's coronation in 1953 each child at Primary School received a long and thick commemorative pencil which had, listed on its cylindrical flank, the names and the reign-dates, in order, of all the Kings and Queens of England. The list started with William the Conqueror and ended with the start of the reign of the present Queen. Sadly the pencil has long gone but it sparked the author's life-long love of the History of England and of its monarchs. But happily, the times, dates and places of birth of many of them have been recorded assiduously.

We know that the author also loves working with Astrology. What could be more suitable that he should write a book combining these two interests? Character Portraits of the suitable-for-most-practical-purposes type were derived following the author's proposed and previously described method of combining interpretations from individual epoch and birth charts. Please note that none of the interpretations are his. Simply, they have been sorted and blended into what is hoped is a readily understandable whole. All points from the interpretations have been included but duplication has been minimised. Importantly, the unpolished portraits are impartial and consist of relatively modern expressions for appreciation and comparison purposes.

We start with Henry II, the first Plantagenet king, and continue, in time order, to Richard III, the last one. Usually, the portraits have uncovered several surprising traits for each king, as we shall see. Supporting reference materials for the portraits included individual, referenced biographies, individual descriptions in the Oxford Dictionary of National Biography and life-and-times summaries for each king, in Wikipedia.

Wirral, Merseyside, U.K., 2013.

CONTENTS

The Plantagenet Kings of England and Their Reign Dates

HENRY II

"Who will free me from this turbulent priest?"

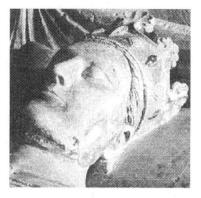

Henry II, the first Plantagenet king of England, was the second child and son of Geoffrey V of Anjou and the Empress Matilda (Henry I's only surviving, legitimate child). Henry was born on the 12th March, 1133 NS at Le Mans, France (see Figure 2). He became actively involved in his mother's efforts to claim the throne of England by the age of fourteen. At age 19 he married Eleanor of Aquitaine, eleven years his senior, the recently divorced wife of the French king, Louis VII. Henry inherited the English throne in 1154 following King Stephen's death. He now controlled an empire that stretched across Western Europe.

Henry was an energetic and sometimes ruthless ruler, driven by a desire to restore the lands and privileges of his grandfather, Henry I. Henry II rapidly came into conflict with Louis VII and fought a "Cold War" with him over several decades, expanding his empire at Louis' expense. Henry undertook various legal reforms in both England and Normandy establishing the basis for the future English Common Law and reforming the royal finances and currency. Henry's desire to control and reform the relationship between the Church in England and the Monarch led to conflict with his former friend, the Archbishop of Canterbury, Thomas à Becket. This conflict lasted for much of the 1160s and resulted in Becket's murder in 1170, for which Henry was blamed widely.

In 1173, Henry's first son, the Young Henry, rebelled in protest at his father's treatment of him and was joined by his brothers, Richard and Geoffrey, and by their mother Eleanor. This Great Revolt was

Figure 1:—King Henry II's Speculative Epoch Chart.

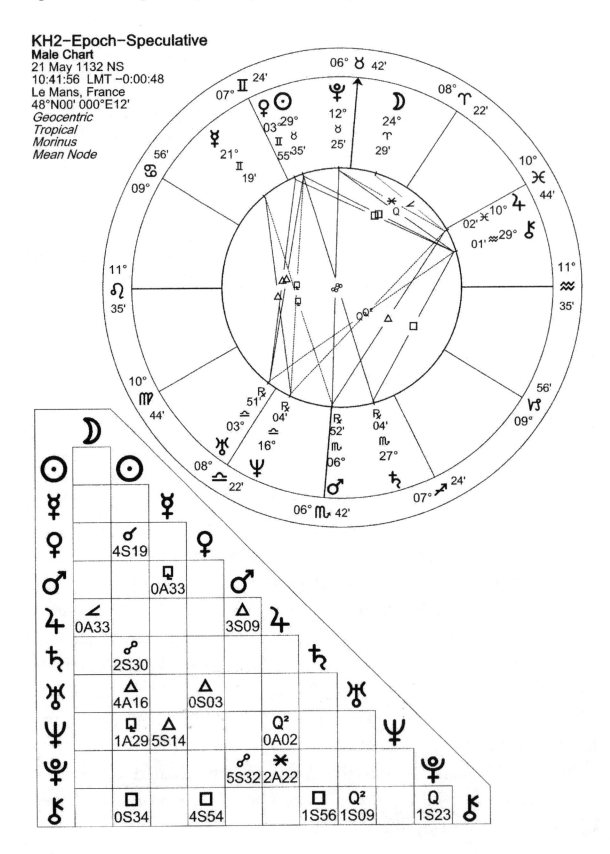

defeated only by Henry's vigorous military action. Young Henry and Geoffrey revolted again in 1183, resulting in the former's death.

Despite invading Ireland to provide lands for his youngest son, John, Henry struggled to find ways to satisfy all of his sons' desires for land and immediate power. Philip Augustus (now king of France) successfully played on Richard's fears that Henry would make John king and a final rebellion broke out in 1189. Decisively defeated by Philip and Richard, and suffering from a bleeding ulcer, Henry retreated to Anjou, where he died shortly after.

Henry's speculative (his birth time is not known) Epoch (see Figure 1) occurred on the 21st. May, 1132 NS, at 10:42. The planetary distribution of the chart is mainly South meaning that he was mostly objective (i.e. concerned mainly with practical and visible things). The overall shaping of the chart is mostly 'See-Saw' showing his indecision but also that his final choices were well-considered. Chiron is at the focus of a fixed T-square showing that he let trying matters remain as they were, causing him strain. Jupiter mediating the Mars-Pluto opposition reveals a do-nothing attitude but a willingness to help others and to contribute to the public's well-being. The Sun in Taurus-Moon in Aries sign polarity shows a strong personality with a tendency to be headstrong, while the Sun in 11th-Moon in 10th House polarity indicates that specialised knowledge would help him to cope with life's abrasive challenges. The Sun (ruler) in opposition to Saturn shows that his self-expression was hurtfully limited whereas the Moon semi-square Jupiter suggests a tendency to be extravagant. Jupiter in the 8th House indicates that his death came as an easy release. The Morin Point in Leo shows a personality that burned for success. Retrograde Mars in Scorpio in the 4th House reveals an active inner life and a tendency to carry grudges.

Figure 2:—King Henry II's Speculative Birth Chart.

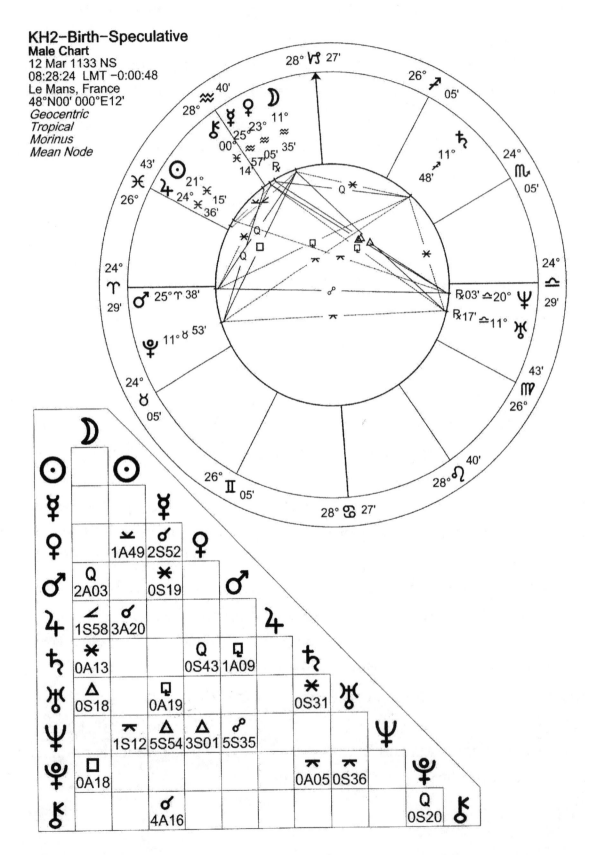

KH2-Birth-Speculative
Male Chart
12 Mar 1133 NS
08:28:24 LMT −0:00:48
Le Mans, France
48°N00' 000°E12'
Geocentric
Tropical
Morinus
Mean Node

Henry's Epoch generates his Ideal Birth chart (see Figure 2) in which the planets lie mainly to the South and East showing both objectivity and that his destiny was mainly in his own hands. Altogether the two charts contain six quintile family aspects indicating good intelligence. Overall the chart shaping is mainly 'Splay' revealing a unique individual with powerful life-emphases. There is a distorted (Yod) kite with Pluto at the focus in Taurus in the 2nd House indicating a well-integrated personality containing both stress and ease for whom wealth and permanence assumed considerable importance. The Sun in Pisces-Moon in Aquarius sign polarity shows ability for business and for large scale pursuits, while the Sun in 12th-Moon in 10th House polarity suggests that he could have helped to make the world a better place for people to live in. The Sun conjoint Jupiter suggests contentedness and good luck. Strong aspects to the Moon from Saturn, Uranus and Pluto show a willing acceptance of duty, a desire to achieve good through unusual objectives and a liability to upsets and forced new phases, respectively. The Morin Point in the 3rd Aries decanate shows courage, enterprise, impulsiveness and the ability to work hard. Some contest between materialism and religion may have affected his life considerably. Mars (ruler) rising and conjoint the Morin Point suggests daring, argumentativeness and that he was prone to righteous indignation. The decanate ruler, Jupiter in Pisces in the 12th House, conjoint the Sun, suggests sensitivity and success in philanthropic work. Venus retrograde in Aquarius in the 11th House indicates that his desire to help could have been overbearing. It also suggests that he rarely felt settled.

Character Portrait

General: Henry was an unusual mixture of stress and ease. Between these two he had a utilitarian outlook with a love of change. Busy enterprise, coupled with the ability to work hard, was his main attribute. Courage, self-discipline and self-denial, daring ambition, pride and fondness for both power and distinction were all clearly present.

On the easy side he was quiet, retiring and harmless with optimism, cheerfulness and contentment. His wanted to express himself through beauty, the arts and gentle ways but he lacked the opportunity for this and so felt frustrated.

When stressed, he became demonstrative, defiant and dogmatic.

Mentality: Henry's mind was powerful, courageous and enterprising. His fine mental abilities included a good memory, sound judgement and strong intuition. He was thoroughly expansive in genial, kindly and emotional ways with gaiety, fun and teasingly caustic humour, all of which were helpful for socialising. Henry had spurts of interest for religious matters, higher thought and education. He also had a tendency for strong prevision and for idealism in which 'clouds of glory' were to be expected rather than any sort of self-delusion. His ideas and hunches should have been acted on. Although his moods were suddenly changeable, this gave him the ability to throw off the static and start new acceptable ways. Overall he had a tendency to genius combined with leadership and inventive, flashing thought that generated success.

However, he also had a tendency to vagueness and muddles that led to many ideas but poor fulfilment. He felt he would always have the privilege of indulging himself as he chose. When confronted by temptation, he avoided the concrete by day-dreaming. Greedy mentally, he truly had to learn to discriminate to prevent each new beautiful whim from causing more collective disharmony than he could cope with. His dreams may have been unrealistic but his future did depend strongly on how much he clung to his past fantasies. At times, he may even have been deceitful, or have become the object of treachery (e.g. at the hands of his youngest son, John).

Unfortunately, his mind and nervous system could be energised to the point of breakdown leading to headstrong rash action, temper and righteous indignation, all with carping and satirical incisiveness. In this state there was no peace wherever he was. Tense situations often ended forcefully with unhappy results. Realistically, his explosive tendency had to be resisted strongly otherwise it led to a totally uncaring attitude, a determination to be first at all costs and a love of both war and contention.

Lifestyle: Henry was a unique individual with powerful life-emphases; his disposition was shown by his own special tastes. He had a robust resistance to pigeon-holing and showed an awkward certainty in every approach he made to life's problems. Although an intense person, he could not be limited to any single, steady point of application. He had an ambitious personality that burned for success coupled with constructive power, organising ability and a strong moral nature. He experienced an active, inner life and faced each day eagerly in the hope that he would always be as physically and mentally active as he was as a mature, young adult. He felt continually that he was not reaching all that he should so there was no chance for rest.

Henry's inclination was to act at all times through a consideration of opposing views but was capable of unique achievement when a development of unsuspected events arose in life. Overly sensitive to his environment, due to his feeling out of balance with surrounding conditions, he kept adjusting his approach to life, which caused him to waste some of his energies He seemed to be indecisive, the more so as he also had an inclination to let matters remain as they were and put up with them so that he became conditioned to trying circumstances but not without nervous strain. Despite the delay created and the energy he wasted, there was much reserve behind his actions and once his final, well-considered choices were made, he carried out every purpose nearly always successfully.

Henry desired to achieve good through unusual objectives. Being independent, he could not easily accept restrictions or limitations on his life. As a result, his independent experiences kept him apart from his beloved humanity. Probably, he cultivated a convivial social environment to gain the right social image that was important to him. He scattered his affections among so many things, people and experiences that individuals close to him felt thwarted in their own abilities to focus their energies. However, this merely reflected his highly changeable nature. Personal rejection gradually made him become more detached. Rather than forgiving those who hurt him, e.g. Becket and Eleanor, his wife, he buried his anger and continued to carry it as part of his basic make-up, so that, in this way, he became his own worst enemy. Instead of spoiling his whole self, he should have tried to discount those parts of himself that had been keeping him alienated from others. With all the artificialities of life stripped away, he could have become a very lonely person. Despite all this, he was still of much more help to others than he was to himself.

Relationships

<u>Others</u>: Henry needed to feel secure with people but was less sure of himself than he would have wanted others to know. In reality, he was popular and fitted easily into the mainstream of society, charming the people he met. He knew how to indulge people and how to make them feel comfortable, which endeared him to them. Actually, he related better with people whose ages were very different from his own. He gained much strength from older people and tested it out on those younger. He expected a great deal from others and manifested a stubborn desire to make others conform to his requirements. He was an enormous energy drain on others around him as he tended to need

their energy to direct himself. Being enterprising and independent, he preferred his own methods to those of others, even though he was wilful and wrong-headed at times. People may have tried to use him for his skills but he learnt to help only those who deserved it. His preoccupation with financial security gave people confidence that he could help them in their business affairs. They believed that he would serve their interests well because he had so much self-confidence.

Henry needed constant encouragement to do something constructive with his life. He wanted to help others. His deep sense of devotion to others came from his early religious training. It was important for him to know that others considered him indispensable and his useful efforts brought him much spiritual fulfilment. In reality his need to help others was a disguise for trying to earn his way back into favour following a rejection. He never fully expected total intimacy for any prolonged length of time but was contented to know that temporarily, his beliefs and ideas were being accepted. He would have gone miles out of his way (e.g. by doing public penance for Becket's murder) to earn that acceptance.

Henry helped others in their needs so he could depend on them for favours when he needed them. His sympathetic concern meant that he could serve people very well if he chose to. He was sensitive to the predicament that many people face in finding a suitable foundation on which to build their lives. This sensitivity to their needs made him qualified to deal with their problems and was an indication of how much potential there was for him for growth and development. If he had directed his efforts to finding a solution to this problem and had offered himself as a guide whom people could follow, he would have achieved the fulfilment he wanted. This was the underlying motivation in his life but he could have accomplished it in several ways, either through his career or through his private life. In practice, he could have been overbearing in his desire to help others to the extent that he would cause hindrance without meaning to.

<u>Friends</u>: New friends were made often. Henry chose friends who were symbolic parent figures. It was through these people that he blamed one of his parents (father, with whom he may have had a psychological conflict) for all the obstacles he could not surmount in his life. He enjoyed supporting his friends in their careers and the experiences he gained helped him to achieve his goals but family obligations may have restricted him in this.

<u>Family</u>: His parents pressured him to live up to their goals but as he became more self-reliant he no longer needed their approval. Some of his apprehension may have been the result of this parental conditioning that taught him to be reticent about taking on responsibilities unless he was absolutely sure that he could handle them.

Probably, he was pre-occupied with giving his children every opportunity to reach their own needy objectives. He had to be very careful not to alienate them by telling them what to do with their lives. He ought to have established his own priorities and to have been convincing when he was away because he needed their support to perform at his best.

<u>Lover</u>: Henry may have gone through bizarre sexual experiences in his search for that which he had not yet experienced. He was too sensitive to people imposing their will on him but, at the same time, he felt he knew what was best for others thereby resulting in the possibility for conflict in his personal relationships. He did not truly want to be on his own in his life. To win the one he loved he had to show both his independence and his creativity. He wanted to share his responsibilities with those he felt were stronger than himself. As a result it was likely that his partner was older than he was (his wife, for example). Duty stopped full expression of his love but a complementary happiness (sometimes secret) was gained. He was an

asset to his partner, who shared his dreams, and there was prosperity through marriage. He hoped that his partner understood his need to be involved in a career yet he worried because his career intruded on his marriage in that he had to stay away from home more than his mate, his children and others close to him, cared to endure. Because so much of his time and energy was devoted to career interests, he may have had to make concessions for the sake of harmony but probably he would have felt annoyed when pressing developments in his career required his personal attention. He didn't want his mate to distract him because he knew that reaching his goals would have been mutually beneficial and that he had to stay on course.

Career

Early: Henry's destiny lay mainly in his own hands. He would have had plenty of opportunities in life and a feeling that "good luck" was to be expected. Early in life Henry knew what he wanted to accomplish and he wanted very much to fulfil his life-long dreams. Formal education was important if he wanted the advantages that came with success so he tried to get the training he needed. Additionally, his emotional vulnerability made it necessary to get the best possible education to cope with the pressure of competition in getting established professionally. Without the insulating defence that knowledge provides, he may have found that abrasive, challenging situations became overpowering. He needed to remember that "Nothing ventured, nothing gained", so he had to find a way to be more assertive (not too difficult for him!) as he'd already defined his objectives.

Freedom, which was precious to him, could have been achieved by developing his capacity for administration. He also came to know how to promote his ideas to derive the most benefit from them. Success came in life through energy and the desire to excel. He wanted to travel and there was success from abroad. He was fortunate in worldly matters that required enterprise, a daring spirit and a determined will. There was also success in philanthropic work, in things of the sea, and in the arts generally. Thus there was a good chance that success was achieved early in life. However, he felt that external forces were preventing him from reaching his goals so he developed an intense, internal energy to overpower these imaginary enemies to his progress. More negatively, he also had a tendency to squander gains, to be extravagant and to trust to luck too readily.

Henry was more suited for public pursuits than for domestic ones. He had ability for business and for large-scale undertakings where intuition would have been required. He showed willing acceptance of duty and success through orderly and practical ways even though these may have caused him personal limitation and a corresponding lack of gaiety. He would have been a good manager because he was knowledgeable, sensitive and caring enough to achieve his career objectives without burdening the people under him with over-bearing discipline or unreasonable expectations.

Henry could have fulfilled his own needs by using his ability to serve others. Making a contribution that improved the quality of life for others would have helped him to extend his potential.

Middle: Henry tended to have a do-nothing attitude about investing in his future aims because he felt that the world owed him a living. He felt that he didn't have to apply himself if he didn't want to. Yet he helped others in their needs hoping for reciprocity and through his career made his greatest contribution to the public (he initiated legal reforms that established the basis for England's future Common Law and reformed the currency as well as the royal finances). There was gain through adventurous channels in which his ability won high returns, through expected legacies, through uniformed occupation and through unscrupulous financial considerations. His obsession was wealth with a compelling need to achieve permanence. Fortunate materially, he was fitted for a position of success, prominence and responsibility. Both local and national interests attracted him. The important factor here was that there had to be growth potential in whatever activity he chose.

It took a lot of moral fortitude for him to resist the temptation to get what he wanted through collusion or by issuing ultimatums. But with his religious training, or spiritual awareness, he could easily have achieved his goals without resorting to these methods. Probably he had had to work hard to learn as much as he had and he prided himself on being a self-made man. He learnt whom to serve and who should serve him. He understood the power associated with money and he also recognised the social responsibility that this entailed. His intuition helped him to make wise decisions both for himself and for advising others. He placed a high premium on his services and professional skills and he expected to be paid well because he knew he could get the results people wanted. When the price was right he didn't deny himself whatever he could get, either by way of worldly goods or by satisfying his physical desires.

Some conflict between materialism and religion probably would have affected his life considerably (e.g. his relationship with Thomas à Becket, the Archbishop of Canterbury). As a result, he may have suffered from public criticism and opposition. He needed to be prepared for rejection as he rose in his career. Sometimes he felt that he wasn't adequately prepared to fulfil the demands of kingship but probably any such feelings were unfounded. He was more capable than he knew at using the lessons he had learned. He may have complained about all the work that others expected of him, but he wouldn't have changed it if he could. He could have achieved his goal of making the world a better place to live in more easily if he had been able to put aside his survival anxieties and concern himself more with social problems. There was little doubt that he had the ability to relieve many of them.

<u>Late</u>: It would take Henry a great deal of effort and self-reliance to gain independence for his later years. It was essential for him to recognise the necessity of making any sacrifices that were required as he invested his talents and developed his creativity to assure his future security. Once again, he should have focused on striving to reach the goals he had established.

Henry may have enjoyed exploring ancient civilisations.

Appearance and Health

<u>Appearance</u>: Henry was just above medium height, well-built with large bones and muscles that became a square build in middle age. His head was full-sized and round with a florid/swarthy/ruddy complexion. He had grey eyes and light or sandy coloured hair with a tendency towards baldness. He had an upright walk.

<u>Health</u>: Henry had good health, a vitality of spirit that could almost be too intense, physical strength and a strong nervous system so good eyesight, hearing and sense of touch. When run down his head, or nervous system, suffered. He had a tendency to falls, chills and to orthopaedic troubles. Death came to him as an easy release with a feeling of expansion into a new life.

Reference: 'Henry II', W. L. Warren, Yale University Press, New Haven, Connecticut, U.S.A., 2000.

RICHARD I

"I would have sold London if I could have found a buyer."

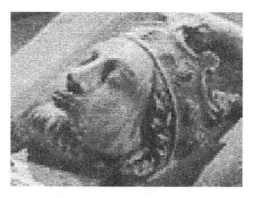

King Richard I of England was known as the Lionheart (Coeur de Lion) even before becoming king because of his reputation as a great military leader and warrior. By the age of sixteen, Richard was commanding his own army, putting down rebellions in Poitou, France, against his father, King Henry II. Richard became the central Christian commander during the Third Crusade and scored considerable victories against his Muslim counterpart, Saladin. The Saracens, who respected and feared him, called him *Melek-Ric*. However, he decided strategically and reluctantly that even if he did retake Jerusalem the Christians would be unable to hold on to it.

Despite speaking little English, spending very little time in England and using his kingdom as a source of revenue to support his armies, he was seen as a pious hero by his subjects. He remains an enduring, iconic figure both in England and in France.

King Richard I (KRI), the third child and third legitimate son of King Henry II of England and the fifth child of Eleanor of Aquitaine, was born on the 15th September, 1157 NS, just after 03:00 p.m. at Oxford, England (see Figure 4). His Epoch occurred on the 10th December, 1156 NS, just after 02:00 p.m. (see Figure 3). The Epoch chart shows that the planets lie mainly to the South and West, which shows his objectivity and that his destiny lay with circumstances and depended on others. The chart's overall shaping is 'See-Saw' indicating indecision but also well-considered choices. The Grand Trine in Air

Figure 3: Epoch Chart for King Richard I.

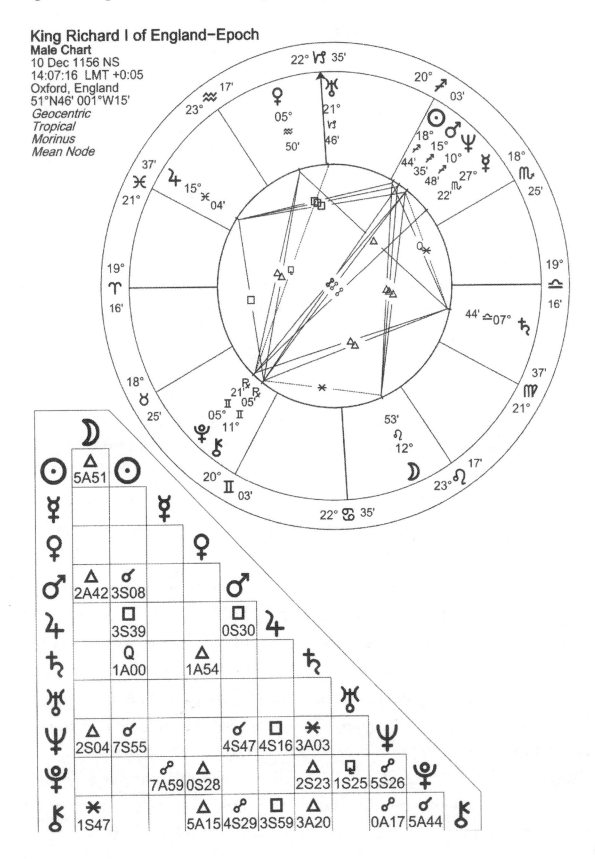

King Richard I of England–Epoch
Male Chart
10 Dec 1156 NS
14:07:16 LMT +0:05
Oxford, England
51°N46' 001°W15'
Geocentric
Tropical
Morinus
Mean Node

comprising Venus, Pluto and Saturn suggests an essentially intellectual and superficial approach to challenges rather than any deep stirring, but passion is provided by the Sun, the Moon, Mars, Neptune and Morin Point all in Fire signs. A mutable T-Square (Jupiter at focus) implies an adjustment to difficulties but not without nervous stress. Notice that Mercury in Scorpio is essentially unaspected (apart from a D^3 [tridecile] to Jupiter) and suggests that Richard could act through sheer emotion without good reason.

Uranus too, has only one weak minor aspect indicating that its principle is not well-integrated with the rest of Richard's personality. The Pluto-Chiron conjunction in Gemini in the 3rd House seems to provide the main focus for the whole chart suggesting that mobility, understanding and support in general would be important to Richard. The Sun in Sagittarius—Moon in Leo sign polarity shows a passionate, spiritual nature, a quick and sensitive mind, and a love of grand surroundings. Much may have been accomplished. The Sun in the 9th—Moon in the 5th House polarity indicates excellent results in enterprises requiring imagination and creativity. The Sun conjoint Mars shows a bold, quick and energetic self-expression and the Morin Point in Aries provides courage, enterprise and the ability to work hard. Overall, the interpretations of Richard's Epoch chart reveal much of the great ability he required to lead the Third Crusade.

His Epoch generates his Ideal Birth chart (see figure 4). There are five quintile aspects altogether in both charts indicating good intelligence. For the Birth chart the North planetary distribution shows subjectivity, the South some objectivity and the East that his destiny lay mainly in his own hands. The chart shaping is either 'Locomotive' or a 'Bucket' with two handles. For the latter, Jupiter lies anticlockwise to the vertical to the Pluto-Neptune rim, and sug-

Figure 4: Ideal Birth Chart for King Richard I.

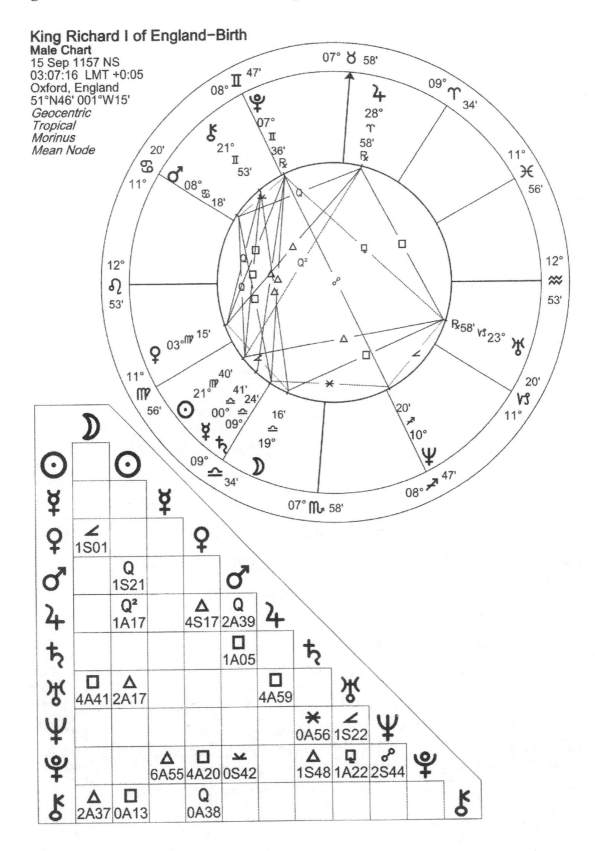

King Richard I of England–Birth
Male Chart
15 Sep 1157 NS
03:07:16 LMT +0:05
Oxford, England
51°N46' 001°W15'
Geocentric
Tropical
Morinus
Mean Node

gests cautious expansion. However, Uranus, lying clockwise to the rim, implies impetuous change. For the former, the locomotive shaping reveals a strong sense of lack, or a need, or of a task to be achieved, or of a problem to be solved, in the social and intellectual world around him. Jupiter, leading this shaping, suggests uncanny skill in uncovering opportunities for exploitation and expansion that favoured his career. Once again, Pluto appears as a focal point for the whole chart and suggests a vital need for friends. Similarly, Mercury is essentially unaspected (apart from a triundecile [U³] to Chiron) enhancing his tendency towards sudden, thoughtless action. Alternatively Mars is quintile both Jupiter and the Sun and shows that he had to act on his plans and noble intentions otherwise they would have become meaningless. The Sun in Virgo—Moon in Libra sign polarity shows independent thought with a talent for writing, quick perception and fine judgement. The Sun in 2nd—Moon in 3rd House polarity reveals his desire for a comfortable life-style, pleasurable activities with close friends and good communication skills. The Sun square Chiron suggests frustrations when attempting to work with friends and allies whereas the Moon trine Chiron shows that security, nevertheless, was important to him. The Morin Point in Leo's 2nd decanate reveals an ambitious and power-seeking personality that burnt for success but with a liability to go to extremes. Jupiter, as the decanate ruler, showed that he understood the value of money and that he prided himself on achieving his goals ethically. However, the square to Uranus introduces a tendency that wilfulness and an insistence on being different produced tactlessness and bluntness that offended others.

Character Portrait

General: Richard was keen on sport, travel and cheerful ways of enjoyment that resulted in contentment with his own surroundings.

His vital need for self-expression was shown energetically: thus bold, forceful, passionate, initiatory, playful, and quick, with an ambition that burnt for success. He was also tenacious, persistent, self-disciplined, self-denying and deliberating. However, there was limitation to all this, probably through his father. He had a strong moral character so that his response to exposure to temptation and to base desires was well-controlled. Although courage, enterprise and the ability to work hard were his main personality attributes, he had tendencies to be showy and extravagant. A liability to go to extremes made him more demonstrative, active and, at times, very rebellious with a resulting weakening of will-power. An inherent tendency to rash action had to be resisted strongly but there was more reason, intellect, mitigated impulsiveness and less sympathy at the expense of more martial elements. He was both objective and subjective as shown by much artistic ability (poetry, writing and music).

Mentality: Proud, alert, with quick perception and fine judgement, Richard combined strong intuition with imagination within a clear mentality. He was inspired, versatile and always searching for more. Being able to sense other minds, he was, at the same time, isolated from them. Self-righteousness permeated much of his thinking coupled with an abounding free-spirit at the instinctive level. He was enthusiastic and 'all out' for far-flung ideas but somewhat exaggerative and off at a tangent. He could have been more imaginative than practical but certainly he wasn't. The philosophical and spiritual side of his nature showed a marked love of change and of argumentativeness as strong characteristics. He had a tendency to be scientific and success came through inventive, flashing thought, while his spiritual nature gave him the ability to foresee and so to prophesy. Thus much was given out through the reception of ideas and influences (e.g. from art generally [but also from a love of the sea]). Yet despite his considerable adaptability for higher mental activities (e.g. religion) he had a feeling of inadequacy here. However, his interest in serious study would have deepened as life went on.

Richard could express his independence of thought, blended with feeling, very well using his talent for writing. He was capable of deep concentration. Finding the proper vehicle for putting his ideas to work presented a very serious problem. His obsession was mobility (both mental and practical) with a compelling need to achieve comprehension. He was fascinated by mysteries and wanted to solve them.

An aptitude for critical repartee, accompanied by drawling, charming speech, friendly discussion and for gazing at beautiful objects was a poorly integrated part of his mental make-up. Similarly, a characteristically intense attitude, tending to the occult and penetrative about the affairs of others, was, again, a poorly integrated part of his mentality.

Being inscrutable, impetuous, always searching for sensation and novelty, as well as restlessness comprised some of his less desirable traits. Fortunately tendencies to be taciturn, utopian and to be irresponsible were usually well-controlled. But he was neither patient nor plodding, with a liability to change and to opinion that fluctuated.

Lifestyle: Richard needed to learn his own personal truths at the most basic level. Being honest with himself was the key to his greatest security. He wanted a comfortable lifestyle that allowed him to develop his many interests.

Richard desired to present an honourable image to the world while maintaining complete freedom of thought and action. He clearly saw the conflict between what he thought the world expected of him and of how he was himself or of how he would have liked to have been. He wanted the best for himself, his friends and for the world he lived in. This caused problems because he saw a great gap between what his ideal was and the prevailing reality. This caused him to become a creature of extremes, vacillating between too much and too little self-assertiveness. He could well have appeared as a rebel.

Richard tended to act at all times under a consideration of opposing views but was capable of unique achievement through a development of unexpected circumstances. However, he was apt to waste energies through his improper alignment with his own surroundings. Additionally he attempted to adjust to difficulties or to by-pass them, though rarely without nervous strain. Thus he seemed to be indecisive but his final choices were well-considered.

Richard showed a dynamic and exceptionally practical capacity. He was moved more by external factors than by aspects of his own character. He was a self-driving individual who was neither strange nor unbalanced but rather was orientated towards power. He experienced a strong sense of lack, or of a need for a problem to be solved, or of a task to be achieved, in the social and intellectual world around him.

Richard continually eliminated all those factors from his life that impeded his internal development and his personal expression. Inner restlessness pushed him to sample all that he had not yet experienced. Unexpectedly, he had moments of acting through sheer emotion without any good reason. He could have been childishly naïve, not seeing the full circumstances, or situation, into which he was jumping. As a result, he often had to pull himself back out. In the process he developed much wisdom that was useful not only to himself but to all he met. He was impatient to achieve and was usually more interested in the final result rather than in the steps that would get him there. He liked being in control, and actually had to be, in order to live out what he believed, regardless of the opposition. His entire life could well have stood for the results that came from one shining achievement.

Relationships

<u>Others</u>: Probably Richard was more generous with strangers than with those who were closest to him. Although he was inquisitive about others, he rarely shared his innermost thoughts with anyone, except perhaps his partner (see lover). However, working closely with people either individually or in groups was particularly suited to his temperament. He had a talent for dealing with people, for inspiring them and for stimulating them to excel in their abilities. He communicated well with people and had the persistence to derive the most minutely detailed information with all the supporting evidence he needed to justify his position. He understood people's problems and they looked to him for the insight they needed in finding solutions. For his part, he had the confidence that his ideas would make an indelible impression on them. Yet wilfulness and insistence on being 'different' produced tactlessness and bluntness that offended others. His views tended to be egocentric so that the ideas and ways of all others tended to be dismissed. "Everyone was out of step but our Richard".

At a higher level Richard had to learn to listen to others and postpone decisions until he was thoroughly informed. He tended to jump the gun when it would have been better to go slow, which wasted precious energy. His dedication to achieving a high degree of competence, coupled with his gift for conversation, should have improved his chances of attracting the attention of important people. He needed to seek out their help because he would have benefitted from their inspiration.

<u>Friends</u>: Richard was vitally interested in neighbours and had a compelling need for friends, whom he was able to influence. There were strange relationships, sudden estrangements and even, possibly, the death of friends. He cultivated friendships with people who were

in a position to help him achieve the security he wanted. He enjoyed social gatherings and pleasurable activities but there was the tendency that his attempts to support and work with friends and allies were frustrating and stressful. His friends probably liked him more than he did himself. Things done for them caused them to reciprocate. Richard took his friendships very seriously and often appointed himself as the conscience of his friends, which could cause great friction. To avoid this, he achieved his goals, dreams and ambitions through them vicariously. In this way he could be of great help to friends but would not be bound to them personally.

Family: Richard was vitally interested in, and gave good support to, close relatives. Their affairs mattered to him. Had Richard had legitimate children (he had an illegitimate son, Philip) they would have delighted him because they would have brought out his ever present youthful vigour and enthusiasm. He would have considered them as stimulants that made him fully exploit his creativity to satisfy their needs. Although he may well have spoilt his children by overindulging them, as he always did with those he loved, he would also have been a disciplinarian because of his concern for their growth and maturation. However, if he had made excessive demands on his children, they may have rebelled. In any event, he might well have lost them as they pursued a life of their own.

Lover: Richard's affections and partnerships were subject to disclosures, upheavals and new starts but with good results in the end. His love nature could go out to many but there was apt to be confusion about this. Probably he fancied himself as quite the romantic lover and generally he tried to live up to his partner's expectations. He tried to find a mate who shared his enthusiasm for the goals he hoped to realise. He felt more secure in a relationship when the lines of communication were open, and any tension that existed could be discussed and cleared up to his satisfaction. Observers were probably impressed by the total companionship he had with his marriage partner. However, any childish naivety on his part would have been extremely difficult for marriage because it would have offered his partner little stability.

Career

<u>Early:</u> Richard's destiny lay in his own hands, in the hands of others as well as depending on the prevailing conditions. His fate was influenced by ambition, emotion and through speculative tendencies. Although his life was vigorous, he had the ability to work hard, push on in life and learn lessons of duty and self-control. However, taking liberties with the law, or relaxing his moral code, could have proved disastrous.

Richard's early conditioning cultivated the firm belief that he could succeed in anything he attempted. His problem was that he didn't always feel inclined to make the effort, so that he may have missed some opportunities. He may have felt that nothing was so urgent that it couldn't be done later and that there would always be other opportunities to show his capabilities[1]. This self-indulgent attitude meant that there would be delays before he could attain the position for which he was qualified, and reaching his goals may have taken longer than usual for someone with his advantages. He may have been one of those who had to fail before he could succeed. His plans and noble intentions meant nothing unless he acted on them. He could be fulfilled only if he invested the time and energy to achieve his dreams with devotion and self-discipline. In addition to satisfying his needs he could have got the recognition his skills and accomplishments deserved. There was no other way he could have got financial security and independence so that he could come and go as he wanted. But a little application would have given him the credentials to become established in his career. He would have had little trouble getting the support he needed in his objectives. He was always eager to promote himself to the world and pursued his ideals with devotion. Plenty of opportunities and good luck were to be expected. Additionally good administration would help him to early success. He had always known that someday he would have the opportunity to pursue the goals he had selected early in life. His crusading temperament was shown by his uncanny skill in uncovering opportunities for exploitation and expansion that formed the basis of his career. Much may have been accomplished and perhaps have resulted in a great figure.

<u>Middle:</u> Richard prided himself on achieving his goals ethically although his emotions mustn't have been allowed to interfere with them as he was easily disturbed when familiar conditions were altered. He understood the value of money and had as much as he needed when he put his resources to work. He was wise enough to get advice about investing in the future. Security was important to him—being informed helped. Any insecurity about the future was alleviated by putting his imagination to work.

Usually he was able to overcome his natural caution about his career but there were times of frustration due to his questioning all that he would like to do against the great scope of his wisdom. Thus, at times, he found himself not acting when wishing he was, or acting when wishing he wasn't.

Richard should have directed more of his energy to programs relating to society at large. He wanted to contribute here as well as amass personal achievements, and personnel changes during his career gave him that opportunity, but he needed to be careful that he didn't become the victim of such changes. Probably he would have been recognised for his social service efforts.

Richard's eagerness to be noticed by important people in his profession was nearly boundless. Despite a tendency to too much reliance on luck he enjoyed excellent results in enterprises that allowed him to exploit his imagination and creativity. He could have been successful in business because he became well-informed about all the details, and he handled them with control. He gave everything to his job, because, in general, he liked his work. He asserted himself forcibly to show that he wouldn't be intimidated by even the most determined competitors. He impressed superiors and helped them to achieve their objectives. He may have had to travel in his business, which he was willing to do, if success and future growth depended on it. However, he had to avoid intimate contact with fellow associates or discussion of his private life.

<u>Late:</u> Richard hated to depend on others. He wanted to retire as soon as possible. With his inspiration this was possible. He wished to be independent so that he could enjoy his later years without feeling obliged to anyone.

Appearance and Health

<u>Appearance:</u> Richard was tall with large bones and muscles that became a square body-build in middle age. He was full-faced with a ruddy complexion, grey eyes and sandy, light hair with a tendency to baldness at the temples. He had an upright walk.

<u>Health:</u> Richard had good health and a vitality of spirit that could almost be too intense. Physically robust he combined excellent strength both physically and emotionally. A good nervous system was important to him because he could become exhausted by his career demands. As a result he may have suffered from intestinal trouble.

- -

References: 1) 'Richard I', J. Gillingham, Yale University Press, London, U.K., 1999.

2) 'Richard the Lionheart—The Mighty Crusader', David Miller, Weidenfeld and Nicholson, London, 2003.

- -

<u>Comment:</u> Richard was like his father but on a slightly larger scale. [1] We wonder how much this aspect of his character contributed towards his decision to withdraw from his intention to besiege Jerusalem and so start the end of the Third Crusade. Did he intend to come back later and finish the task properly?

- -

JOHN

"An Interdict on England is the equivalent of a papal declaration of war."

John, the youngest of five sons of King Henry II of England and Eleanor of Aquitaine, was not expected to inherit significant lands and became known as 'Lackland'. However, John's elder brothers William, Henry and Geoffrey died young so by the time Richard I became king John had become the potential heir to the throne. John attempted a rebellion against Richard's royal administrators while his remaining elder brother was taking part in the Third Crusade. Despite this, after Richard's unexpected death, John was proclaimed king and his continental territories were recognised by Philip II of France at the peace treaty of Le Goulet in 1200. However, shortages of military resources during the next war and his treatment of his continental nobles resulted in the collapse of his empire in Northern France in 1204. John spent much of the next decade trying to regain these lands but was finally defeated by Philip II at the Battle of Bouvines.

John's judicial reforms had a lasting impact on the English Common Law System but when he returned to England after Bouvines he faced a rebellion by many of his barons unhappy with his fiscal policies and with his personal treatment of them. Both sides agreed to the Magna-Carta Treaty of 1215 but neither complied with its conditions. John died (after an excess of peaches) whilst on campaign during the rebellion in eastern England, late in 1216.

An argument with Pope Innocent III had led to John's excommunication in 1209 but the dispute was settled by John in 1213. Today John is usually considered as a "hard-working administrator, an able man and an able general". Nonetheless, he is said to have

Figure 5: King John's Epoch Chart.

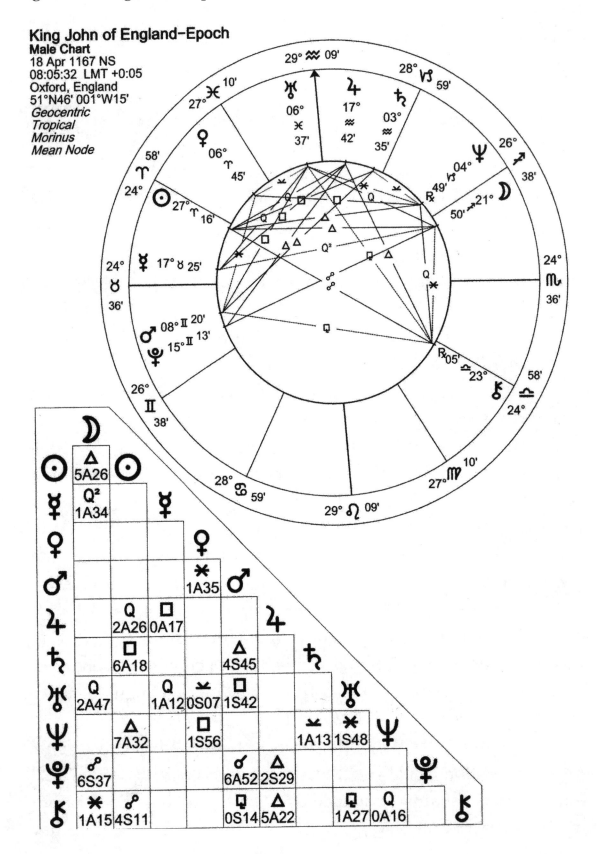

King John of England–Epoch
Male Chart
18 Apr 1167 NS
08:05:32 LMT +0:05
Oxford, England
51°N46' 001°W15'
Geocentric
Tropical
Morinus
Mean Node

had distasteful, even dangerous personality traits including pettiness, spitefulness and cruelty.

John was born on the 31st December, 1167 NS at just before 17:00 at Oxford, England (see Figure 6). His Epoch occurred on the 18th April, 1167 NS (see Figure 5). His Epoch chart shows that most of the planets lie above the Morin Point, i.e. to the South, indicating objectivity, but also more to the East than the West suggesting that his destiny lay more in his own hands than in those of others. The overall shaping is a 'Bucket' with the Moon opposite Pluto as the rim and Chiron in Libra in the 6th House, opposite to the Sun, as the somewhat anticlockwise handle. This suggests a particular direction to his life-effort in which he provided cautious support to others, with difficulty, but to which the response was favourable (Chiron sextile the Moon). There is almost a Grand trine in air involving Chiron that suggests an intellectual but superficial approach to difficulties. The Sun in Aries—Moon in Sagittarius reveals a quick, sympathetic and spiritual nature with a tendency to go to extremes, whereas the Sun in 12th—Moon in 8th House polarity shows his incredible insight into what motivated people. The Morin Point lies in the 3rd Taurus decanate and indicates a cheerful, friendly personality that inclined to be too easy-going. The ruler, Venus in Aries in the 11th House shows that he was happy among like-minded friends and that he had an unusual, intriguing expression of love (exact semisextile to Uranus). Mercury rising in Taurus shows that his speech and gestures were smooth with some skill in telling tales but the exact square to Jupiter shows carelessness, indiscretion and poor judgement. This aspect indicates a lack of good working between the liver and the nervous system and may well lie at the root of these poor mental qualities. On the other hand, Uranus is bi-quintile to Mercury and to the Moon implying excellent and inspirational intelligence.

Figure 6: King John's Birth Chart.

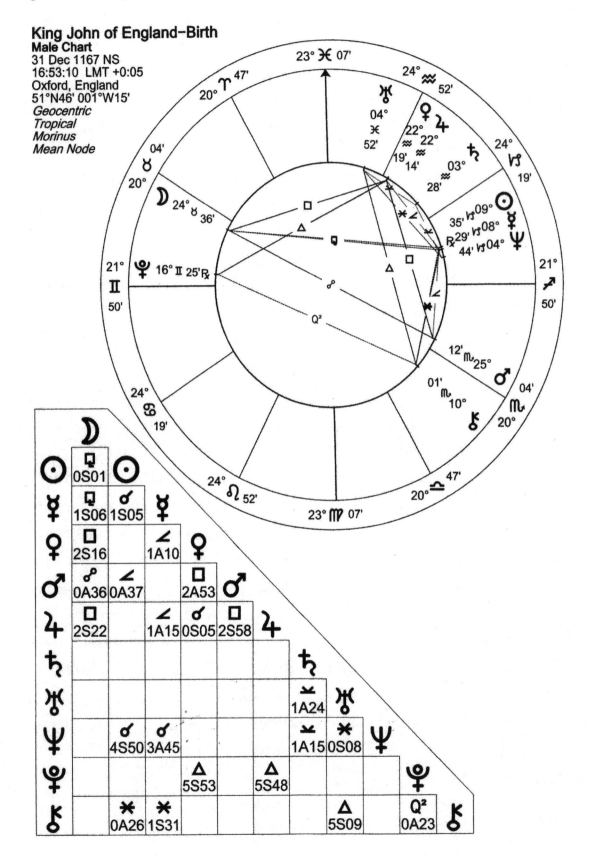

King John of England—Birth
Male Chart
31 Dec 1167 NS
16:53:10 LMT +0:05
Oxford, England
51°N46' 001°W15'
Geocentric
Tropical
Morinus
Mean Node

John's Epoch generates John's Ideal Birth chart (see Figure 6). Altogether there are six quintile family aspects in these charts indicating good intelligence. For the Birth chart the planets lie mainly in the South West confirming objectivity and showing a destiny that lay mainly in the hands of others and/or depended on prevailing conditions. The 'Bundle/Bowl/Bucket' shaping shows a bunching of interests, idealism, an ability to make much out of little and possibly impulsive elimination (Pluto as the very clockwise handle). A fixed T-square, with the exact Venus/Jupiter conjunction as the focus, shows an inclination to let difficulties remain as they are, but not without nervous stress. Saturn and Mercury, with its conjunction to Neptune, occupy bi-semisextile, bi-semisquare and bi-sextile positions in the SW quadrant indicating his ties to the general public, his worry about any partner's gold-digging tendencies, and his need to watch out for his ethics, moral standards and for 'clever' individuals, respectively. The poorly aspected Sun in Capricorn—Moon in Taurus polarity shows conservative ambition, firmness and self-control but marred by poor feelings, impatience and faithlessness. The Sun in 8th—Moon in 12th House polarity indicates a need for a good education, for self-analysis and for deferred marriage until he was well-situated. The Sun exactly sesquiquadrate the Moon suggests a cleavage in his life relating to parents or to early childhood (imprisonment of his mother after the 1173 rebellion). The Sun strongly semisquare to Mars shows bad temper and the strong sextile to Chiron indicates that he gave favourable support and charity. The Moon closely opposite to Mars reinforces bad temper and the square to the Venus/Jupiter conjunction reveals a lack of peace at home together with extravagance and a liability to trust to luck too easily. The Morin Point in the 3rd Gemini decanate shows a quick wit, mental ability and a search for literary and scientific knowledge. The ruler, Mercury retrograde in Capricorn in the 8th House reveals a weighty thinker, who found difficulty expressing his exact meaning. The decanate ruler, Uranus in Pisces in the 9th House shows well-intentioned changefulness and strong intuition. Retrograde Pluto, rising in Gemini, indicates a powerful inner drive, a lack of contentment, a search for novelty and a thirst for experience. Notice, finally, that the exact conjunction of Venus with Jupiter in Aquarius in the 9th House shows that love was unemotional and detached but that harmonious relationships existed with women and young people. It shows also that his artistic inclinations were strong and that he evinced a scientific spirit.

Character Portrait

John had a strong and harmonious nature that may well have been marred by poor feelings, impatience and faithlessness. Although a generous, cheerful, friendly and humanitarian person, he easily became sceptical, inscrutable, moody, quarrelsome and pugnacious. There was ambition, intellectual quality and reason but also an inclination to run in a groove or to become too conventional thus making for a laborious and over-cautious approach. He could be adhesive, strongly intuitive, obstinate and plodding, yet he had a thirst for experience, a magnetic, robust self-sufficiency and, at times, an adventurous/courageous personality with great potentialities. He bunched his interests, gathered them to himself and acquired an ability for gaining wealth and the power to do good with it. More negatively he had tendencies to be extravagant and to trust to luck too easily. Although objective his artistic inclinations were strong with some musical skill (he had a good voice). He also inclined to the spiritual, the mystical and to affairs connected with the sea.

Mentality: John was very changeful, and all with good intent, but too much at the mercy of his emotions. His quick, sympathetic and emotional nature had a tendency to go to extremes. On the one hand his speech, thought, gesture and movement were slow and smooth with some skill in weaving tales. As a deep and weighty thinker, he rarely made the same mistake twice. His self-expression was difficult because he tried to pin-point his exact meaning. Thus he tended to talk about meaningful, serious or sober matters. His communications in personal affairs was approached rationally and coolly with unconsciously accurate speech and prophesy about the future. Yet, on the other hand, due to his changefulness his expression could suddenly become quick, dramatic, exaggerative, hasty, impulsive and chattering.

John's mentality was active, sensitive and able, seeking both literary and scientific knowledge wherever he could find it. His mind was not that resilient but turned towards practical, pleasant and selfish things. He sought sensation, inventiveness and novelty all impetuously. His obsession was mobility (mainly mental but also practical) with a compelling need to achieve comprehension. He sought self-expression through unconventional, scientific and humanitarian ways. In addition he had a tendency to the intangible. Overall, he had an intellectual but superficial approach to difficulties. Changeful and irresolute he was given to enthusiasms that did not last but plenty of energy and determination were used while he was in the mood. He tried to convert his ideals into actuality by his unusual power of leadership in spiritual, scientific and appreciative ways. His persistent mind tried to exercise firmness and self-control but his mind was over-widened (probably due to a liver problem [see Health]) so that he lost grasp, producing careless woolly-thinking, indiscretion and poor judgement. His unfortunate inability to concentrate properly made it difficult for him to focus on an objective. Probably his inspirational ideas were better well-scrutinised.

Lifestyle: John did not live a spontaneous life because he was much more in tune with the purpose of his own thought patterns than with the natural flow of forces in the world around him. In all things

41

he considered the end result before even contemplating the steps he might have taken towards achieving it. He tended to be highly pragmatic and practical. He dipped deeply into life and poured forth the gathered results of his experiences with unremitting zeal. His life was held within certain narrow bands of opportunity being 'inhibited' rather than 'scattered'. He was able to convert little into much by taking small beginnings and building them into great ones. There was a particular and rather uncompromising direction to his life-effort (see Career) with no desire to conserve himself or his resources. He could have been a splendid leader in the affairs of the world with vision and readiness to change old ways. In fact he was awkward, if not in a position to lead. There was a love of pleasure and social life that helped to bring popularity but a tendency to be too easy going could have led to difficulties unless it was firmly controlled. He was unready for, and hated to submit to, the confinement of a daily routine because it limited his freedom, but he wouldn't have been free really until he had applied himself and earned it. Additionally he had an inclination to let difficulties remain as they were, and to put up with them, thereby becoming patiently conditioned to trying circumstances but not without nervous strain.

He had to keep a watchful eye on his ethics and moral standards to make sure he didn't unwittingly erode his position before the public. Similarly, he had to keep a sharp eye out for clever individuals who tried to entice him into schemes that weren't within the bounds of legality. He was sufficiently afraid of the consequences that he was unlikely to resort to lax moral behaviour or questionable ethical standards.

There was a powerful inner-drive that motivated him. He was rarely content and extremely difficult to please because what he was seeking was usually beyond the grasp of those who tried to help him. He analysed everything and everyone that caught his attention, including himself, because he was intensely curious to know how and why people were motivated. His fascination with the unknown led him into little known areas of inquiry. The knowledge then available probably was insufficient to give him the information he required to answer his questions.

John had a life-long quest to purify himself. His constant urge to seek brought him through many intense experiences. Early on he could well have gone through paranoid periods in which he got bogged down in his own depth but was more than able to plod his way back out. Sometimes, he thought he was alienated from society and possibly he could have become the product of increasingly magnified destructive thoughts. He needed to learn how to transform his past visions into more appropriate forms that complied with constructive actions of his own time. No sooner had some of his past thought become established, than he was then prepared to absorb more knowledge for future planning.

Impulsive during youth he became more introspective after mid-life. Then, instead of wanting to impress himself upon the world, he sought to understand how much he was a product of the world. He was serious about faith and beliefs. He was interested in examining all kinds of subjects; the deeper and more profound the better. He never accepted answers to his questions on a superficial level but sought to know the ultimate why of all that exists. He continually retraced the deepest meaning he could find to all he perceived. His thought processes went right to the heart of life's essential meaning and he may have experienced sexual problems because the depth of his thinking made him question often the value of all physical expression.

Relationships

John's subordinates (the barons) were likely to have been quarrelsome, but otherwise John had a desire for harmony with others in a widespread way. Popularity and much social life were likely to result from the widening of the scope of his desire to form harmonious relationships with others. This would have applied to women and to young people especially. He was good at achieving smooth working of any club or society to which he belonged. As a friend to others he reaped their loyalty by return.

Generally, John was successful in dealing with the public[1], who relied on his ethical behaviour in handling their affairs. In this, he was rather gifted. The rapport he had with people made them feel comfortable and confident that he could help them. People usually sensed that they could tell him their troubles and he would do what he could to help them overcome them. Thus, he felt for others, understood their needs, was sensitive to their failings and would have helped them by elevating and improving them if he could. Accordingly, he developed incredible insight into what motivated people to act as they did. It became painful for him to know so much about people, because it suggested that he had an obligation to use his creativity to solve their problems.

Few people could deceive John successfully because he was intuitively alert to dishonesty and insincerity. He would do almost anything for those who were honest with him. He knew the steps that must be taken to achieve anything substantial from his previous experience and tried to convey this to those who were always looking for the easy way out.

Personal relationships constituted John's greatest difficulty as others tended to lose patience with all he was trying to build. However, he became more easily understood later in life after his thinking had found suitable outlets in society. He should have listened carefully to the advice he gave to others because this very advice would have turned out to be for his own guidance later on.

<u>Friends:</u> The essential energy of John's social life usually ensured many friends. He was happiest among those who were like-minded.

<u>Family:</u> Although warmth and enthusiasm entered into relationships as expressed to young people in a family, there was a lack of peace, harmony as well as an uneasy expression of affection in John's home.

<u>Lover:</u> John's unusual expression of love (or in artistic accomplishment) or in any kind of partnership was unemotional and detached but delightful, intriguing and fascinating. He easily slipped away from one attraction to form another. Thus, partings were likely but for good reasons and with pleasant replacements or reunions. Initially warmth and affection were strong, keen and ardent in sexual relations but tended to be self-seeking. Basically he was too cool; friendship was preferred rather than emotional ties. He developed a tendency to shy away from intimate relationships. Even when he was involved, he kept much of his thoughts to himself, while silently observing the meaning of all that which surrounded him. His love affairs were numerous and he was better in partnership than alone. Overall partnerships and lovers were disappointing, undependable and involved both secrecy and confusion.

He might have had problems in relationships because he attracted people who made excessive demands and expected him to comply with them. Additionally his partner would have admired and respected his efforts although he might have thought that he would be accepted only to the extent that he provided every possible material comfort. Moreover, his partner may have required much attention and he may have had to compensate for his partner's problems while getting established professionally. He should have deferred marriage until he was reasonably settled in his career. Probably his eventual mate was as highly developed as he was and shared his destiny, but his career may have caused some problems if she had resented the time and attention he devoted to it. Marriage and other relationships were difficult because his inner turmoil made him continually uproot and transform his needs, basic desires, concepts and learning. However, in reality, his true progress always came from after-the-fact realisations.

Career

Early: John's fate depended on his early environment because there was less power to break away from early training and parental influence. There was a cleavage in his life relating to his parents, which affected his whole life (the consequences for his mother following her rebellion in 1173) so that generally he was influenced by guardians and friends but the resulting disharmony in his nature could well have urged him to accomplishment. Earlier he did things the hard way but this would have helped him to achieve later on. Probably he became impatient to grow up because he was anxious to prove that he could succeed if given the opportunity. Overall his destiny was in his own hands, in the hands of others and dependent on prevailing circumstances. Additionally, travel, exploration, life abroad and dealings with foreigners would have been favourable.

John's childhood circumstances gave him the opportunity to develop without psychological problems so that, as he matured, he would have been able to integrate the various forces within himself. He had to get a good education to make a worthwhile contribution to society, which is what he wished to do. This was critical so that he could show his professional abilities. There were indications for success in studying any of the more profound subjects. Rather than assume that he couldn't have done something, he should have got the training that would have qualified him to succeed in it. All his potential meant little unless he willingly invested the time and energy to develop it into a skill that the public would want. However, it was easy for him to neglect this task in favour of more self-satisfying activities. Once he had gained the credentials he needed he probably would have become a specialist. As such he was willing to work hard to gain the approval of his fellow professionals.

John disliked working at ordinary jobs that didn't place sufficient demands on his talent. He wasn't particularly fond of menial tasks either, so he preferred a career that allowed him to grow and develop according to his particular abilities. Mental occupations (e.g. teaching and preaching) and diversions would have attracted him. He preferred a career that provided social advantages that others enjoyed as well as a substantial return for his services.

John had an ability to adapt to circumstances—good or bad—that would have persisted throughout his life. His ability to succeed was strengthened by his basically harmonious nature that enabled him to handle conflict and frustration before they grew into a major crisis.

John had to find ways to translate his imaginative ideas into worthwhile activity. Considerable sacrifice was required as he had to work hard at converting his potential into skills before he could develop them because he knew he could make a contribution by applying them later. He knew exactly how to reach his goals but he had to stay within his limits to avoid disappointment. At the same time, he had to extend himself to the maximum. He got his cue for his goals from people he admired when he observed the benefits they enjoyed. He would have made sacrifices to acquire similar luxuries.

John gave cautious support, help and charity under work conditions, which could have involved difficulties but he received favourable responses. Probably he should have chosen a profession requiring his incredible insight into what motivated people. His ability to handle people and their problems offered him many opportunities for professional success. A service oriented profession would have suited him well. However, he had to learn to work to serve the needs of others, i.e. investing his creativity in helping others fulfil theirs.

In the beginning he had to focus his attention on individuals who needed assistance and learn from them how capable he was. Lack of self-confidence kept him from taking on large scale programs but that changed as success reassured him of his competence. His growth became assured, because he would have committed himself to serving the public. This is how he would have made his best contribution (and gained security for his later years).

Middle: John was most effective when he applied his skills in a professional capacity as he was definitely tied to working with and for the general public. He was guided by firm standards and in his personal dealings he insisted on fair play and justice. He adapted his allegiances to lines along which he could make his efforts count for the most. Self-control and organising power would help in which chastity would have been a keynote for success. Further education would have given him enormous leverage to promote better government and a better society. He may have measured his own worth by how well he succeeded before the public. Some suitable outlets for his talents included financial and/or psychological counselling, physical therapy, medicine and its branches. A career in institutional work as in correctional facilities, homes for the mentally, physically or elderly handicapped would also have been suitable for him. Educational and social programs would have offered him opportunities for self-expansion and success.

John looked around for people whose needs or situations required his skills to improve them. He communicated freely to people that he was willing to help them with their problems. His skills were urgently needed by those people in society who were most lacking in resources. However, "seedy" elements in society held little interest for him but these were precisely the people who most needed his ability to intercede for them with persons in high places. He had a deep spiritual obligation to the people he served and he couldn't afford to disappoint them. His spiritual responsibility to others distinguished him. When someone appreciated a service he had done, his vitality was regenerated. He placed a high premium on his services because he knew how valuable they were so he should have enjoyed deservedly high rewards for his efforts.

John went to great lengths to gain acceptance in a social environment that would have improved his social standing. He might even have indulged in social politics if it would have improved his social standing.

John had always to keep his moral and ethical standards in focus to make sure he didn't unwittingly erode his position before the public. It would have been so easy for him to assume that the ignorant deserved to be "taken" by anyone who was better informed. He needed to remember that he had a social obligation to the public and that he could have been held legally responsible for any deception he practised. He also had to be careful not to distort his objectives by a lust for personal gain, because that power could have become destructive.

John was a professional. Not content just to be proficient in his skills he looked for new ways to apply his talents. He readily got involved with the problems of his environment so he was probably quite aware of what was needed to solve them. He may have underestimated his ability to take command in such efforts yet he would have known that many people needed help. He may not have taken action personally but at least he would have alerted the proper authorities and aroused public support by speaking out against offensive socio-political conditions.

John experienced exciting, new and sudden happenings abroad but also frustration when travel plans were being arranged. Although he had difficulties with foreigners, or with journeys carried out for duty, his contacts were better when the foreigners were elderly. Seriousness and concentration, along with controlled, rationally thought-out aims, paradoxically seemed to demand much freedom for their accomplishment. Thus long-term results could have been good if duties had been realised after efforts had been made.

Appearance and Health

<u>Appearance:</u> John was of middle stature with dark brown hair and a dark tawny complexion. He used his hands cleverly.

<u>Health:</u> John had good health with more vital energy than stamina but this wasn't absent either. His tendencies to excesses would have weakened his health. Although much may have been achieved his tendency was to overstrain through overdoing with a resultant liability to minor accidents. There was a lack of good working between his liver and an otherwise responsive nervous system. This may have been at the root of some of his poor mental behaviour.

- -

Reference: 'King John', W. L. Warren, Yale University Press, London, 1997.

- -

[1] On this basis, were John's real opponents confined only to the barons?

- -

HENRY III

"If the papal prelates knew how much I, in my reverence of God, am afraid of them and how unwilling I am to offend them, they would trample on me as on an old and worn-out shoe."

Henry III was the first child king of England since the reign of Æthelred the Unready. He assumed the crown under the regency of the popular William Marshall, 1st Earl of Pembroke, but the England he inherited had undergone several drastic changes during the reign of his father, King John. He spent much of his reign fighting the barons over Magna-Carta and the royal rights, but was eventually forced to call the first "parliament" in 1264. England prospered during his reign and his greatest monument is Westminster, which he made the seat of his government and where he expanded the abbey as a shrine to Edward the Confessor. Unfortunately, he was unsuccessful on the Continent where he endeavoured to re-establish English control over Normandy, Anjou and Aquitaine. He is the first of only five monarchs to reign in England for fifty years or more.

- -

Henry, the first child and elder son of King John and Queen Isabella of Angoulême was born on the 8th October, 1207 NS speculatively (the actual birth time is not known) at just after 16:30 (see Figure 8). This birth time and its corresponding Epoch appear to describe what little is known of his appearance and pious character. The Epoch occurred on the 28th January, 1207 NS at 17:45 (see Figure 7). The planets in this figure lie mainly to the East showing that his destiny was in his own hands. The overall, irregular 'Splay' shaping

Figure 7: King Henry III's Speculative Epoch Chart.

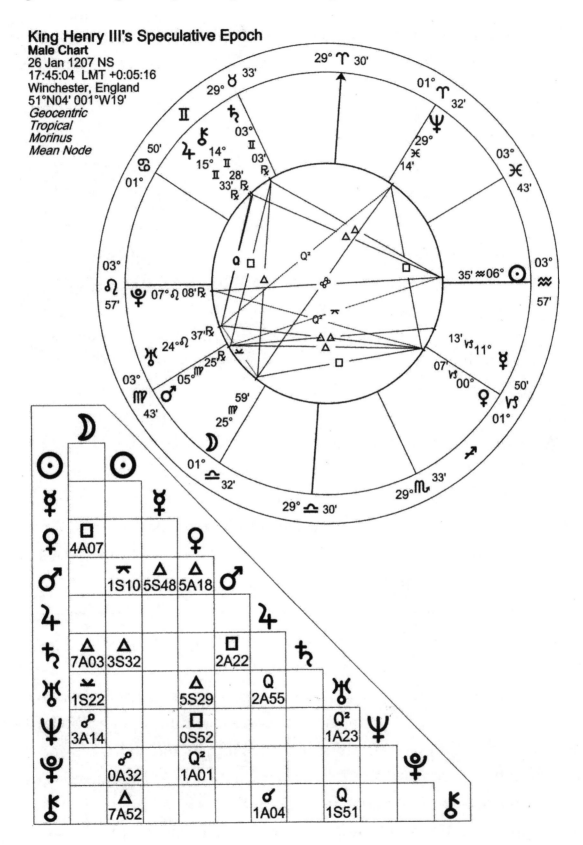

shows the awkward certainty in every approach he made to deal with the difficulties in his life. The chart also shows a mutable T-square, having Venus, just in Capricorn, in the 6th House as the focus, bi-square to the Moon-Neptune opposition. The T-square shows an adjustment to difficulties and an attempt to by-pass them but not without nervous stress. There is some mediation to Venus here from the trines to Uranus and Mars in the 2nd House. Notice that Mercury has only a weak trine to Mars, which suggests that this part of his mentality would not be well-integrated with the rest of his personality. The Sun in Aquarius—Moon in Virgo sign polarity shows a love of hygiene, science and intellectual pursuits. By itself it also shows that he would have prospered best in association with an enterprising partner. The Sun in the 7th—Moon in the 3rd House polarity reveals the ease with which he got involved with people and his enjoyment within the mainstream of human activity. The Sun (ruler) strongly opposite to Pluto rising in Leo suggests that he advanced himself through ruthless behaviour towards others but, at the same time, made more compromises than he should have. The Moon opposite to Neptune implies good sensitivity with possible good fulfilment despite tendencies to escapism, to deceit and to self-gullibility. The Morin Point in the 1st Leo decanate indicates an ambitious and power-seeking personality and so gave him his spirit of enterprise. Pluto rising in Leo shows stimulated self-confidence, even megalomania, and a need to achieve fully-creative self-expression. Its opposition to the Sun shows how important his privacy was to him. The quintile to Venus indicates trouble in love affairs.

The Epoch generates the Ideal Birth chart as given (see Figure 8). There are six quintile aspects altogether in both charts that attest to his intelligence. For the Birth chart itself the planets lie mainly to the West showing that others and prevailing conditions would contribute to his destiny. The planets, as at Epoch, have a 'Splay' shaping that

Figure 8: King Henry III's Speculative Birth Chart.

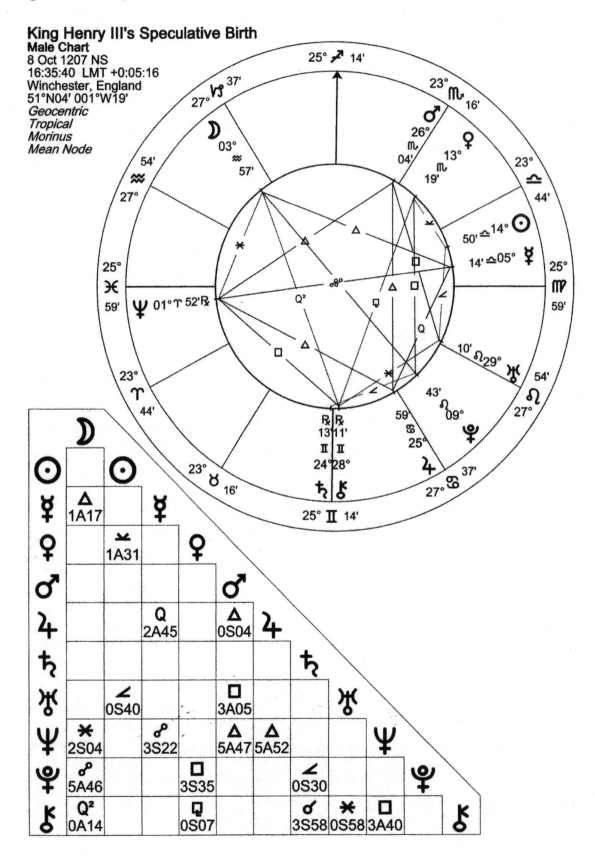

King Henry III's Speculative Birth
Male Chart
8 Oct 1207 NS
16:35:40 LMT +0:05:16
Winchester, England
51°N04' 001°W19'
Geocentric
Tropical
Morinus
Mean Node

reinforce the individual/purposeful emphases in his life. The Grand Trine in water between Neptune (ruler, rising and so focal point), Jupiter and Mars shows a struggle for universal harmony and probably a pleasant person whom others liked to help. The Sun in Libra—Moon in Aquarius sign polarity implies splendid foresight for humanitarian principles and a kind, gentle disposition. The Sun in 8th—Moon in 11th House polarity indicates his preoccupation with finding the right area for him to apply himself to. The Sun semi-square Uranus indicates self-insistency leading to brusqueness whereas the Moon, strongly trine to Mercury, shows a good, commonsense mentality, and the exact quintile to Chiron in the 4th House reveals that the response to his support and help in home affairs was quite favourable. The Morin Point in the 3rd Pisces decanate shows a strongly artistic personality with an impractical tendency to concentrate on visions of the future. His pride caused him trouble and his psychic qualities could have proved unhealthy. The ruler, Neptune, rising retrograde in Aries and the Grand-Trine focal point, indicates his spiritual nature, his sensitivity and how easily he could be influenced to submit to people and to situations. Neptune rising in Aries could have imparted a smooth, even semi-transparent skin, to Henry.

Character Portrait

General: At his best Henry had an ambitious and power-seeking personality that burned for success. His self-confidence, faith in his own ideas, pride, desire-to-rule, passions, managing ability and a dramatic instinct were all stimulated. He showed a thirst for experience verging on the sensation-seeking, great potentialities, a robust and harmonious personality that was also magnetic, adventurous, courageous, inscrutable, self-sufficient and sceptical. Additionally, there was a love of hygiene, practicality and business ability.

Henry experienced some limitation to his self-expression, possibly from his father, but he became conditioned to this so that wisdom, patience, and constructiveness grew and brought success in later life. On the way he tried to adjust to difficulties and to by-pass them though rarely without nervous stress. Generally his disposition was kind, gentle, reserved, controlled and humane yet sociable and friendly. Sometimes he was too unresisting, yielding, changeable, elusive, whimsical and indolent but never when principles were at stake. He also had a self-willed, self-insistent, revolutionary streak that was awkward, inflexible and disruptive. This could lead to unbridled impulses. When frustrated and dissatisfied, pride in his personal qualifications was apt to carry him beyond the limits of the fear of consequences making him hard, harsh, unfeeling, suspicious, brutal and even foolhardy.

Henry had a strongly artistic personality, possibly containing an interest in the psychic, the mystical and the occult. He had a tendency to be impractical because he concentrated mainly on visions of the future rather than on those of the present. Perhaps selfishness, jealousy, conventionality and materialism were developed also.

Mentality: Henry's mind was capable of concentration, common-sense and nervous force. He was original, inventive, intuitive and possessed a good memory. He exhibited neatness, precision, carefulness and critical faculties leading to a love of science and of intellectual pursuits generally. He had an inflated self-awareness and sense of mission that was responsive to direct inspiration and to radical ideas with the power to propagate them. He also had the power to psychometrise along with the ability to judge human nature. He would have had splendid foresight for humanitarian principles, large businesses, associations and public companies. Thus his good sensitivity could have been brought to good fulfilment despite tendencies to escapism, to deceit and to self-gullibility.

That part of his mentality that showed good, energised seriousness was not well-integrated with the rest of his personality. Possibly he had aversions, forebodings and perverted ideas that made him moody, absent-minded, procrastinating, full of schemes and plans, subtle, tricky and subversive.

Constantly he lived in a state of illusion. Continually he imagined himself in different identities as he kept trying to displace a constant feeling of loneliness. Earlier he had begun to imagine himself as different from his ideas of himself. Whether he had consciously realised it or not, this was the beginning of his spiritual journey. He would have sacrificed old parts of his identity until he had truly blended with his higher spiritual nature. Much of his life then took place at the subconscious level as he kept sifting through his formless nature trying to establish a concrete sense of belonging to himself. Like a chameleon he was in a continuous sense of change, always readjusting himself to the environment he was in at the moment.

He tended to feel sorry for himself, always believing that something was missing in him that might have been found in another person. However, he could have overcome this feeling as soon as he could have accepted the formless part of himself as his true nature, understanding that this gave him the freedom to blend with his environment so that his true identity was more spiritual than personal. He would have learnt that all of life is but appearance, including the image he had of himself.

Lifestyle: Henry had an intensive personality that couldn't be limited to any steady point of application. He was inclined to be impersonal yet particular in his interests. He tended to be awkward in every approach he made to life's problems. Similarly, there were highly individual, or purposeful, emphases in his life during which his temperament became noticeable according to his own very special tastes. For example, his privacy was very important to him so that few people who knew him violated it because he could become vindictive. He preferred to be left alone but would nevertheless fight for his rights if anyone tried to obstruct them.

Henry was on a life-long quest to purify himself. His constant urge to seek brought him through many intense experiences. Impulsive during youth, he became more introspective after mid-life. Then, instead of wanting to impress himself on the world he sought to understand how much he was a product of the world. There was a powerful, inner drive that motivated him. He was rarely content and extremely difficult to please because what he was seeking was beyond the grasp of those who were trying to help him.

Henry saw the world-shift in values (that had begun in England during his father's reign) as a personal crusade during which he was to play some intrinsic part. Personally he questioned his identity in terms of what he himself was doing to make the world more meaningful. He tried to project a sense of secure strength, built on honest foundations, to a world that sorely needed it. He felt an obligation to overcome all that had ever made mankind weak. Thus he spent his entire life with one goal in mind: to develop power, first over himself and then, by example, over the false structures in society that needed more creative and honourable foundations. In other words, he was engaged on an enduring struggle for worldly harmony.

Relationships

<u>Others:</u> Although Henry had a strong tendency to advance himself through ruthless behaviour towards others thereby making many enemies resulting in deprivations and sorrowful experiences, generally he was perceived as a pleasant person whom others liked to help. People usually sensed that they could tell him their problems and he would do what he could to help them find solutions. People sought his advice on important matters because he had such good

insight, so a career here would have been a good choice. However, although he understood people's needs and was sensitive to their failings, he was easily influenced to submit to people and to situations. He made more compromises than he should because he assumed that others would make similar concessions to him. This was ill-advised. Unconsciously, he was saying that he was less competent than others and so had to give in to them. His uncertainty here then made others apprehensive about dealing with him. To avoid unpleasantness he often withdrew. With his potentially easy-going personality he needed to have been more aggressive. This was especially so when he tried to make beneficial personal contacts with people whom he admired for they might have stimulated his development. At the same time, and on the other hand, he was upset by people in important positions who had distorted social values.

Henry enjoyed being in the mainstream of human activity and he had a talent for getting people to support him in his enterprises. His ability to succeed was enhanced by the ease with which he got involved with people. They approved of his plans and he trusted that these would satisfy their needs. In turn, he was generally eager to reciprocate when people needed his help, which benefitted him in his long-range goals. He knew how to use opportunities that came through others and how to derive the greatest yield from them, sometimes exceeding the rewards enjoyed by those who had made the opportunities available.

<u>Friends:</u> Henry was fortunate to have such a high level of comprehension that he got something of value from every communication with his colleagues or friends. However, he had to be wary of friends who gave him advice because they might not have understood him at all. He was easily intimidated by his friends' achievements. But they had applied themselves and were only getting what they deserved. His future could have been as satisfying as theirs,

if he had accepted the fact that there was more to life than indulging in pleasures.

Family: Probably Henry was more demanding than other members of his family, expecting more favours than they got, and not being particularly appreciative, either. Early in life he was conditioned to concentrate on his own family and endure the sacrifices required to help them. Once freed from this situation he should then have invested in his own future so that he would have had security in retirement. Although there was a tendency of danger to his children, the concentrated support, help and charity that he provided in home affairs was received very favourably.

Lover: Sensuous, Henry had a powerful sexual drive coupled with the desire to be the dominant partner in all relationships whatever their nature. His affections and partnerships tended to include unrestrained (and even perverted) love affairs that were subject to disclosures, upheavals and new starts with trouble and unpleasantness. Nevertheless, social and sexual success was likely throughout life, bringing pleasure and material gain. Possibly he formed a permanent relationship early in life. Actually, marriage and other relationships were difficult for him because his inner turmoil made him attempt continually to uproot and transform his needs, basic desires, concepts and learning. However, his true progress always came from after-the-fact realisations.

Henry respected his own and his partner's needs and ambitions and he worked very hard to convince his partner that he cared when it probably wasn't necessary. She already gave him all the support he needed to expand his area of responsibility. If he and she had complemented each other, then both of them would have been supported in reaching his goals. She recognised how important his goals were to him and shared his desire for a comfortable and secure lifestyle. Additionally, if she had been equally fascinated by change and progress, then he would have been very happy. Partnership, karmic marriage and legacies would have had a major financial impact—mainly good but occasionally bad.

Career

<u>Early:</u> Henry would have had a changeful life, a fluctuating future and many struggles. His destiny was in his own hands, in the hands of others and also determined by prevailing conditions. His early years made a deep impression and forced him to rely on his own resources. If he had been delayed in getting his career underway it was probably because he couldn't decide which area would give him the greatest return for his efforts. He was deeply preoccupied with finding an area that would give him security in his later years, rather than one that permitted him to exploit his creativity fully. He may have needed to back up a little and re-examine his motivations. He might have discovered that his creativity could have satisfied certain needs of the larger society. He had many opportunities for applying his skills where they were most needed. When he focused on providing a service that made demands on his creativity then his future security would have come as a natural bi-product. If his goals had been defined clearly then all he needed to realise them was to get an education. He certainly knew that without training his objectives and future goals were greatly limited. He had to evaluate his goals carefully and make plans for achieving them. It would have been a good idea to meditate on his objectives, which could have been buried deep in his subconscious.

Probably he was disorientated when he first made the transition from dependence to security and independence. A career allowing self-determination would have given him a say about his own progress and growth. A routine job was not for him because it would have denied him the full development of his potential. Although he did have his own initiative, activity and hopefulness, he may have prospered in association with, or under the control of, another supplying these qualities, in which case he would have been willing to work thoroughly. Journalism, writing, broadcasting, communications, law, politics, government service, social science, vocational guidance and teaching would have been appropriate for him, would have allowed him to apply his talent and so let him make a worthwhile contribution to society.

Middle: Henry was determined to succeed in his ambitions and gain independence. His goals were very important to him and he worked hard for the public support he needed to achieve them. He had to be careful not to distort his objectives by a lust for personal gain, for that power could have become destructive. When someone appreciated a service he had done his vitality was regenerated. Nothing was more satisfying than knowing that he had helped to make the world a better place for everyone. Because he rarely looked back, his future rewards were limited only by the commitment he was willing to make to them.

As an idealist deeply appreciative of philosophical or spiritual matters, Henry was pained to see how little was done to improve the quality of life for many people in society. His compassion went out to those who were sociologically and economically locked into unfortunate situations. Formal education allowed him to give professional attention to these social conditions. He had a certain inclination for politics in which he could have succeeded if he had had the proper training in government and law. He may also have been drawn to speculative investment but there was a tendency to losses here. In either case he needed to be as well-informed as possible so that he wasn't deceived or misled. However, with his creativity, he could have gained a secure place for himself in society.

<u>Late:</u> Henry dreamt of a more abundant way of life and he wanted to make the most of his basic resources so that he could satisfy his anxieties about the future. He wanted to enjoy a more leisurely life in his later years.

Appearance and Health

<u>Appearance:</u> Somewhat tall with large bones, muscles and broad shoulders, Henry developed a square build in middle age that was a little slighter than might have been expected. He had an upright walk. His hair was light in colour, his eyes grey and his complexion was pale, delicate and possibly even semi-transparent.

<u>Health:</u> Generally Henry would have had good health and a vitality of spirit that could have been almost too intense but which could have been marred by blood diseases and by nervous exhaustion. This latter was brought on by alternating morbid depression and exultation. Additionally his psychic tendencies may have been unhealthy and difficult to understand. Moreover, unusual, chronic diseases were possible but unlikely to be life-threatening.

- -

Reference: 'King Henry III of England—A Short Biography', W. Hunt, 2011.

- -

EDWARD I

"It is easy to beget sons, but the loss of a father is irredeemable."

The first son of Henry III, Edward sided with the barons supporting the Provisions of Oxford in 1259 during his father's reign. After reconciliation, he was captured by the barons following the Battle of Lewes in 1264. He escaped after a few months and defeated Simon de Montfort, the barons' leader, at the battle of Evesham, the following year. After the rebellion, Edward left on a small crusade to the Holy Land but on his way home in 1272 he heard that his father had died. Making a slow return, he was crowned two years later.

Creditably, much of his reign was spent reforming royal administration, common-law and establishing parliament. However, his attention was drawn to military matters. After suppressing a minor rebellion in Wales in 1276, he responded to a second rebellion in 1283 with a full-scale war of conquest. He built castles and towns in Wales, filled them with Englishmen and subjected Wales to English rule. Following a Scottish succession dispute, Edward claimed lordship over Scotland and fought a war that almost defeated the Scots. Unpopular taxation was levied to fund his wars. By the time that Edward died in 1307, he left his son, Edward II, an ongoing war with Scotland as well as many financial and political problems.

Edward I (nicknamed 'longshanks') had been a tall man, temperamental and intimidating. He has been criticised for his uncompromising attitude to the barons, his brutal conduct towards the Scots and by his ruthless expulsion of the Jews from England, in 1290. However, his subjects respected his medieval ideal of kingship as a soldier, administrator and as a man of faith.

The eldest child of King Henry III and Queen Eleanor of Provence, Edward was born on the 24th June, 1239 NS at half-past eleven at night, at Westminster, London (see Figure 10). His Epoch occurred on the 14th October, 1238 NS at 10:35 (see Figure 9). His Epoch chart shows that the planets lie mainly to the South indicating objectivity. The overall shaping is 'See-Saw' suggesting indecision but also well-considered, final choices. Essentially, there is a Grand Trine kite in air with Jupiter, in Aquarius in the 2nd House, as its focal point. This means that Edward made a superficial, intellectual attack on his problems rather than a deeply stirring one. This Grand Trine kite is mediated stressfully by a cardinal T-square that has Pluto at its focal point. This reveals an intention to surmount life's difficulties. Notice that Pluto lies midway between the Sun and Mercury and is conjoint to both. Notice also that Uranus, at one arm of the T-square, opposite to Saturn, lies in Capricorn in the 1st House and thereby becomes an important, personal planet. This suggests inspired leadership. The whole combination of Grand Trine kite and cardinal T-square shows that Edward's personality was well-integrated. The Sun in Libra and the Moon in Virgo sign polarity shows a critical personality softened by an ability for comparison that was useful for business affairs, especially when combined with special aptitudes for finance (Jupiter) and for leadership (Uranus). The Sun in the 11th—Moon in 10th House polarity indicates emotional vulnerability making training/education essential. The Sun semi-square Venus shows an irresponsible inclination towards beauty and ease but also the importance for honourable achievement. The Moon opposite Chiron suggests that the response to his efforts of support at home was unfavourable. The Morin Point in the first Capricorn decanate shows

Figure 9: King Edward I's Epoch Chart.

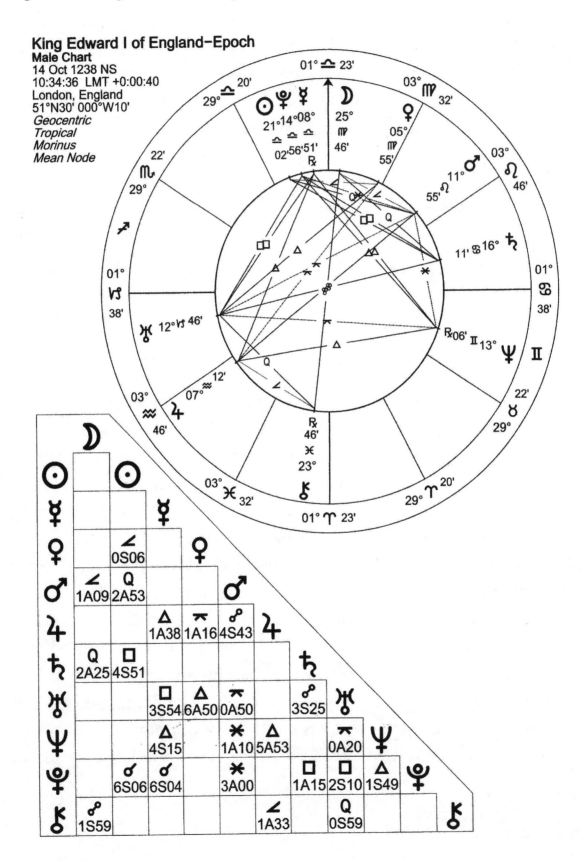

King Edward I of England—Epoch
Male Chart
14 Oct 1238 NS
10:34:36 LMT +0:00:40
London, England
51°N30' 000°W10'
Geocentric
Tropical
Morinus
Mean Node

a persistent, self-controlled personality while the ruler, Saturn in Cancer, setting in the 7th House, suggests ambition but also misfortune. Retrograde Mercury in Libra in the 10th House reveals that he was apt to reflect on past achievements, that his thought was parent orientated and that people close to him hardly understood him. However, Mercury trine Jupiter shows a witty mentality and a deep respect for the value of money. Uranus opposition Saturn shows that he wanted a strong-minded, but considerate mate.

His Epoch chart generates his Ideal Birth chart (see Figure 10). There are seven quintile aspects altogether in both charts signifying intelligence. For his Birth chart the planets lie mainly to the North indicating subjectivity, while the overall shaping of the chart, once again, is 'See-Saw' reinforcing the 'indecisive but well-considered' interpretation given for his Epoch. This time, there are two cardinal T-squares that strongly reinforce the Epoch's interpretation that he intended to surmount his life difficulties. Notice that Chiron, rising in Aries, is bi-quintile Uranus and the Neptune/Mercury conjunction, as well as the focus for one of the cardinal T-squares, i.e. Chiron's bi-square to the Sun and to the Moon. All this suggests that he tried to provide thoughtful support at home and to friends but that this proved difficult. Notice also that Pluto is the focus of the remaining cardinal T-square (containing Uranus and Saturn) indicating that he was greatly concerned about his resources (but he intended to surmount this problem!) The Sun in Cancer—Moon in Capricorn sign polarity shows a practical and ambitious attitude, suitable for business, whereas the Sun in 4th—Moon in 10th House polarity indicates difficulty maintaining an equal relationship with his parents. The Sun opposite the Moon shows his doubt that he could succeed in his career but that the disharmony in his nature would urge him to accomplishment. It also reveals his dilemma about whether he could cope simultaneously with both his career and his

Figure 10: King Edward I's Birth Chart.

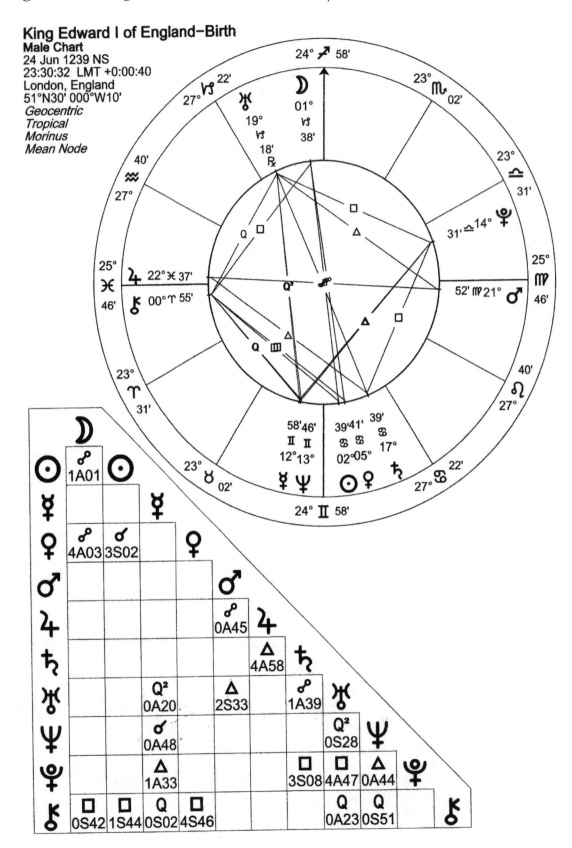

King Edward I of England—Birth
Male Chart
24 Jun 1239 NS
23:30:32 LMT +0:00:40
London, England
51°N30' 000°W10'
Geocentric
Tropical
Morinus
Mean Node

home life. The Morin Point in the 3rd Pisces decanate suggests impracticality in that he preferred to concentrate on visions of the future rather than on those of the present. Neptune, as the chart ruler reveals sensitivity and, in conjunction with Mercury, shows a highly impressionable mind. Pluto, the decanate ruler, in Libra in the 8th House, suggests that he knew that he would stand strong eventually. It also suggests that his death would occur in a public place. Jupiter, rising in Pisces, shows overly imaginative, emotional ways, his kind desire to help others and his tendency towards strong religious beliefs.

Character Portrait

General: An attractive personality, Edward expressed himself through beauty, art and gentle ways, although somewhat too irresponsibly and lazily. Genial, jovial, kindly, optimistic and mirthful, his emotional ways showed his deep feelings as well as an interest in psychic matters. Success came through exercising his cheerful, humorous, studious, deserving and witty personality. Any lack of determination or strength of will was countered by inner stability and assurance, by self-discipline and by serious, practical abilities. Ambitious, with a craving for adventure, excitement and the unusual, he showed self-assertion with a vital need for power and independence. Both objective and subjective, his well-integrated nature could read character well, was also critical but which was softened by a strong ability for comparison. He demonstrated adaptability, opportunism, social instincts and a love of justice. Also he desired wealth and wanted to acquire and accumulate both money and property. All these traits combined to give him a strong aptitude for business.

On the negative side, he could be dictatorial (always right), avaricious, harsh, brutal, perverted, unscrupulous, fatalistic and eccentric thereby effectively concealing any suggestion of effeminacy. His psychic abilities would have been difficult to understand.

Mentality: Broad-minded yet refined, receptive yet outspoken, and capable of deliberating, penetrative concentration there was little doubt that Edward was clever. Words such as original, intellectual, sharp, quick, inspirational, intuitional, imaginative, critical and zealous were all appropriate for him. Sensitivity and impressionability made a mind that could take varied patterns like wax takes an imprint.

Initially over-imaginative through a lack of commonsense with everyday affairs and through emotions too easily stirred to exaggerative expression, Edward tended to confuse thinking with feeling and became fearful of self-expression. Although there was the possibility of exercising some control over his volatile emotions, he ran the risk of self-repression causing subsequent depression. As a result he had difficulty determining his own identity but by putting himself in one person's place, and then in another's, etc., he came to appreciate situations from all possible points of view.

Edward experienced personal unhappiness because he felt obliged to live up to his own mental expectations. Mostly he tried to establish feelings of mental competence that became his main vehicle for self-confidence. Silently, he tended to underrate himself and so tried hard to compensate. His feeling of inadequacy contributed to his insecurity. This made it more urgent that he asserted himself, even at the risk of having occasional setbacks or reversals. As a result he strengthened his integrity. He wanted to convince himself that his thoughts were constantly creating a direction towards worthiness.

Refined, shrewd and deliberating Edward combined good mental abilities with special aptitudes for generating finances and for excellent leadership through brilliant ideas. His sharp, outspoken and critical intellect sought fulfilment through fantasy-loving, mystical and inspirational ways. Clever and original, he sought new and interesting methods even if this meant letting go of the old. He presented an essentially intellectual approach towards problems that was superficial rather than deeply stirring. However, he did intend to surmount life's difficulties but in reality his mind was led towards physical and practical matters that gave him good intuition for business.

Lifestyle: Edward had a persistent, self-controlled personality capable of achieving success through hard work. He was not accustomed to having his ideas frustrated. Overly repressed, he was prone to holding to himself alone all that which was cherished, whether it was family or knowledge or valued collections. He was all he had got and he was determined to make the best of it. His pride in personal qualifications was apt to carry him beyond the limits of the fear of consequences, which tended to make his nature hard and unfeeling. At times he was extremely contrary, probably because he valued tact and diplomacy more than truth. He was ready to alter his life at too short notice. Even so, there was an added tendency for him to be impractical in that he concentrated more on visions of the future rather than on those of the present.

Edward's obsession was impartiality with a compelling need to achieve harmony. Accordingly he carried out a vital search for the meaning of life with a tendency to become anarchical and compulsive. He held strong religious beliefs, which were the reason behind his deep, spiritual need to help people by using his creativity. He was deeply disturbed by unethical behaviour both in government and privately. Secretly, he yearned for the power to alter many conditions, and he wanted a greater part in determining the future of society.

Relationships

Others: Edward attracted attention from important and influential people. They would have recognised his abilities even if he didn't.

Companionable and hospitable, Edward could take his place among large groups as easily as among individuals. People usually felt comfortable with him because he made them feel important. He learnt something from everyone he contacted, yet people close to him hardly understood what he stood for. Being directionally unsure himself, he was always interested in how people from the past would have approved, or otherwise, of his present decisions. He could have accomplished a great deal when he used his innovative ability to serve the needs of people he dealt with. However, if he had wanted his ideas and suggestions to win greater approval, he may have had to make some sacrifices to show that he understood other people's problems. He was impatient with people who didn't have the courage to stand on their own and felt that everyone had to live according to their own code of behaviour.

Edward overflowed with kind desire to help others. It may have been difficult for him but he must not have lost his own identity through trying to help others. But he also had to realise that others' needs had a high priority and that his personal desires may have had to come second. However, he experienced an unfavourable response to the support, help and charity he tried to give to others.

<u>Friends:</u> Enlisting the help of friends in his programs gave Edward the necessary energy to pursue them. However, he must have been wary of taking on any obligations to help his friends unless he knew they were willing to pay for his services.

<u>Family:</u> Parents, heredity and family influences played a very important part in his life, more so than usual. Edward had strong family ties and even if he had moved away from his birthplace he would have returned often to renew old ties. He was very attached to home and family but, unfortunately, he found it difficult to maintain an equal relationship with both parents. His head told him one thing

but his heart told him something else, which resulted in divided feelings. If he had preferred one parent to the other, the resulting guilt would have kept him in a quandary and made it difficult for him to establish his own identity. Leaving home may have been necessary and it would have given him time to work out the problem and develop a more objective perspective. He may have decided that being on his own was best for everyone concerned. The psychological realignment had to continue though, since his attitude probably persisted in other relationships.

Edward had grown up with a great need to impress others and yet, at the same time, his self-expression was inhibited by his training in propriety, prudence and caution. Sometimes he wished to be independent of his parents but found it impossible despite not getting on with them, or when separated from them. He experienced conflict with them and as an adult kept thinking that he had to create harmony with them. This he extended to everyone he met. All his levels of thought were parent orientated. Although he had a strong need to reabsorb past understandings that had come from his father, he shouldn't even have bothered trying to live up to his father's expectations unless they coincided with his own.

Edward was idealistic about parents and home but there was an uneasy expression of affection and a lack of harmony there. His home was often a substitute one and strange conditions applied to it. His inclination to provide thoughtful/idealistic support, help and charity at home (and to friends) could have been fraught with difficulty as well as being unfavourably received due both to his domestic and career situations.

Edward's dilemma was to cope with the demands of his career and still satisfy his family's needs. Possibly he would have felt guilty about not doing everything that he could in both areas. Perhaps he was taught that his most urgent priority should have been to his family. Thus his career might well have caused some problems in his marriage because he may have had to be away from home more than his mate and children cared to endure. He must have had to establish his priorities and to have had to be convincing when he was away, because he needed their support to perform at his best. At least, he inspired his children to assert their own identities.

Lover: On a personal level Edward was quite uninhibited in seeking to satisfy his physical needs and sexual appetite. However, there was frustration and disappointment to be expected from others in close connection, whether in marriage or business. They brought responsibility or losses. He might even have been interested in a trial marriage before making a binding contractual agreement.

Edward had an inability to express his internal feelings. His biggest problem came in relationships because he wanted someone who would have shared everything with him. He was uncomfortable as a loner and he needed the support of the one he loved to make his achievements, and his success, meaningful. Yet he also wanted a strong-minded mate who would have permitted him to be himself. He would never have allowed her to dominate him. She must have had to share his dedication to the goals he'd set for himself and must have had to support him even when his career intruded on their relationship. In fact, he would have become very impatient if she had ever become non-committal about their relationship.

Career

Early: In the beginning, if he hadn't been adequately trained, he would have been intimidated by those in authority, which is the main reason why he must have got an education to qualify him for the growth he sought in his career. He was conditioned by his early environmental circumstances to feel obliged to the people who had provided him with the necessities of life. His emotional vulnerability had made it essential for him to get the best possible training so that he could cope with the pressure of competition in getting himself established. Without the insulating defence that knowledge provided he might well have found that abrasive, challenging situations became overpowering.

Edward's parents had given him the training he needed to achieve his objectives by using his creativity. Although some of his remaining apprehension may have come from their conditioning, which taught him to be reticent about taking on responsibilities unless he was absolutely sure that he could handle them, he had to remember that, "Nothing ventured, nothing gained." In addition, heavy career demands may have made him doubt that he could succeed but his competitors had the same anxieties. Hence he had to find a way to resolve his doubts by establishing his goals, seeking them aggressively and then become more assertive. He was able to realise his future goals and objectives when he applied more energy to making careful plans. He should have developed his talent to the utmost so that he could accept any challenge knowing that he would succeed. In this way he was strengthened by building up his ability to stand on his own two feet. His greatest development came when he reached out beyond the narrow confines of his early environment. Self-analysis would have been required for this process. Thus, travel was likely. He knew that in the long run he would stand strong on his own merits.

Edward was more suited to a public life than to one within his family. He sought a field of professional activity that would allow him to make a worthwhile contribution to the future and to humanity. Probably, he showed excellent leadership through his brilliant ideas. Consequently he might have considered a career in public relations, government service, business management, sales or politics. A career in education, working with children or young people, would have been suitable for his temperament. The important factor was that there had to be growth potential in whatever career he chose.

There had been a cleavage in his life relating to parents or to early childhood but the resulting disharmony in his nature could have urged him to accomplishment. He could have been old for his years early on and then returned to them later on to create his future. Probably, he resented the frustrations he had felt in his early years. His fate was affected by his moral growth, by his power to organise and by his ability to rise above the difficulties of his early childhood. Some position of trust or responsibility advanced his interests and according to the self-possession, tact and prudence he displayed, he advanced, made progress and thereby gained recognition, fame and honour. Many obstacles would beset his path and he might well have endured long periods of misfortune but his ambitions were keen and he had acquired a great love of fame and of a desire both to lead and to govern. To summarise, he faced a struggle to help, to assert himself and then rise to power.

Middle: When Edward was on his own, he would have learnt to assert himself, to accept occasional setbacks and to take on the challenge of competition. He would have become independent and secure only by accepting his responsibilities. He was very important to those he served in his career, which is where he should have focused his efforts. He wanted a permanent position and he got it. If he hadn't established a firm base, it may have been difficult for him to achieve his goals. His argument was that he didn't want to get 'locked-into' a situation that would have inhibited him.

He was fully aware that he had to achieve his objectives honourably. He knew how to capitalise on the knowledge he had gained so that he could be proud of his accomplishments. He also knew how to promote his creativity when there was pressure in his career so that he always had a solution to his problems. He was quick to respond to opportunities in his career. Probably his skill and talent were sought-after by his superiors, who knew that he would live up to, and even exceed, their expectations. With power and position came responsibility and he knew that his gains could be overcome by losses unless he lived up to the public's expectations. Through his efforts he could have helped to determine the evolution of social conditions.

Edward would have felt most secure and comfortable working at home, or at least in familiar surroundings. He sought constantly to categorise his knowledge so that it would be ready for use whenever he needed it. He was apt to reflect on past achievements to see how they measured up to all his expectations. He tended to build his future in just the same way as he had built his past. His concern was always to find direction in life. Ultimately he judged most of his success in terms of his ability to display wisdom to others.

Partnership, marriage legacies and possibly inheritance from his parents would have had a major financial impact—sometimes good and sometimes bad. Edward had a deep respect for the value of money but he also understood that he had to maintain sound ethical standards when dealing with the public otherwise correctness would have been missing from his material gains. He had the ability to generate finance for humanitarian and scientific causes unconventionally.

Health

<u>Appearance:</u> Edward was of middle height (wrong, despite Jupiter rising!) bony and thin, and tending to stoutness later. He had a high forehead, pale complexion, full eyes, with a long nose, dark, plentiful hair and was moderately good-looking.

<u>Health:</u> Although a prolonged life was indicated, Edward was susceptible to both chronic illness and unusual diseases. In addition, accidents, nervous disorders, unhealthy psychic tendencies and even paralysis were all possible. Restless, he had a nervous system that

was exposed to all that touched it. Possibly there was depression due to him having to exercise control over his easily stirred emotions. Although he was talkative, times of quiet and withdrawal were needed. As a result he had to plan his actions carefully so that he couldn't have been in danger from nervous exhaustion by pushing himself too hard to meet deadlines.

There is an indication of an unfortunate death in a public place.

Apparently Edward I inherited 'blepharoptosis' from his father, Henry III. Interestingly, they both have 25^0 Pisces as their Morin Point at birth. Would Richard II have had similar trouble, born 130 years later? He had his Morin Points at 28^0 and 26^0 Pisces at Epoch and Birth, respectively.

Comment: Because he was a Plantagenet, tall and showed military prowess, Edward was linked with Richard I. However, their character portraits are markedly different. It seems that the link doesn't stand up to more detailed examination.

- -

References: 1) 'A Great and terrible King: Edward I and the forging of Britain', M. Morris, Hutchinson, London, 2008.
2) 'Edward I', M. Prestwich, Yale University Press, New Haven, U.S.A., 1997.

- -

EDWARD II

"As to the fealty we are certain that we should not swear it;
nor was it ever asked of us at that time (1303)."
At the renewal of the alliance of perpetual friendship with
Philip V of France, in Paris, 1320.

Between the strong reigns of his father, Edward I, and of his son, Edward III, the reign of Edward II was considered to be disastrous for England, marked by alleged incompetence, political squabbling and military defeats. Rumoured to have been either homosexual or bisexual, he fathered at least five children. His inability to deny even the most grandiose favours to his male favourites (firstly Piers Gaveston and later Hugh Despenser) led to political unrest and his eventual deposition.

Edward II's army was devastatingly defeated at Bannockburn, 1314, freeing Scotland from English control and leaving the North of England unprotected.

Edward II is remembered also from his probable death in Berkeley Castle, allegedly by murder, and perhaps surprisingly and importantly for being the first monarch to establish colleges at Oxford and Cambridge: Oriel College at Oxford and King's Hall (later Trinity College) at Cambridge.

- -

The youngest and only surviving son of four, and the last and possibly either the fourteenth or sixteenth child of King Edward I and Queen Eleanor of Castile, Edward II was born on the 2nd May, 1284

Figure 11: King Edward II's Epoch Chart

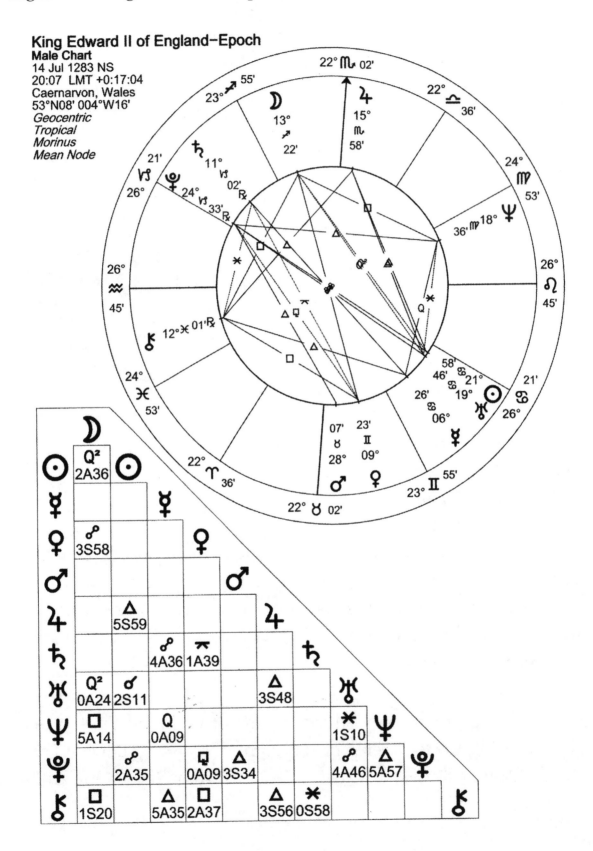

King Edward II of England–Epoch
Male Chart
14 Jul 1283 NS
20:07 LMT +0:17:04
Caernarvon, Wales
53°N08' 004°W16'
Geocentric
Tropical
Morinus
Mean Node

NS, at Caernarvon, Wales, at 08:15 (see Figure 12). His Epoch occurred on the 14th July, 1283 NS at 20:07 (see Figure 11). The Epoch chart shows that the planets lie mostly to the North and West indicating subjectivity and that and that his destiny was governed partly by circumstances. The overall shaping is 'See-Saw' suggesting indecision but also good final choices. There is a mutable T-square having Chiron at its focus indicating stressful attempts to adjust to problems but mediated beneficially by the trine to Jupiter and possibly by the sextile to Saturn. Mars has only one isolated aspect suggesting a potential lack of personality integration of its energy principle and the Sun is conjoint Uranus in the 6th House indicating independence, magnetism and originality. The Sun in Cancer—Moon in Sagittarius sign polarity shows an active personality with a constant yearning for the unattainable whereas the Sun in the 6th—Moon in the 11th House polarity reveals that his developed habits proved resistant to change. The Sun/Uranus conjunction opposite to Pluto indicates a tendency to advance himself at the expense of others while the Moon biquintile to Uranus suggests a tense emotional response. The Morin Point in the 3rd Aquarius decanate confirms his independence and even eccentricity, intellectual interests and a disinclination towards marriage, even though this could well have been beneficial to him. The ruler, Uranus in Cancer in the 6th House shows clever ideas at work of the craftsmanship type and the sub-ruler, Venus in Gemini in the 5th House, opposite to the Moon, reveals his overly demonstrative fondness for his close friends. The close nonile of Venus with Uranus shows the unconventional, tense and unstable nature of his partnerships.

His Epoch generates his Ideal Birth chart (see Figure 12). Notice that there are six quintile aspects altogether in both charts signifying good intelligence. For his birth chart the planets lie mainly to the East and to the South showing that his destiny lay mostly in his own

Figure 12: King Edward II's Birth Chart

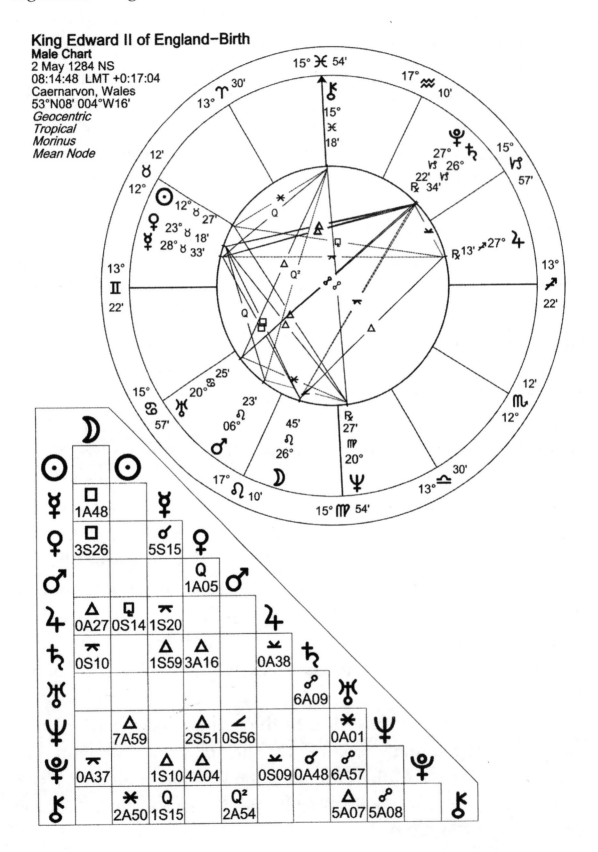

King Edward II of England—Birth
Male Chart
2 May 1284 NS
08:14:48 LMT +0:17:04
Caernarvon, Wales
53°N08' 004°W16'
Geocentric
Tropical
Morinus
Mean Node

hands and that he was more objective than subjective. The overall shaping of the planets this time is 'Splay' indicating an individual with his own special tastes and an awkward personal certainty to every approach he made to life. Notice that the Pluto/Saturn conjunction probably is the main focal point of the chart and suggests serious responsibility through the affairs of others both sexual and financial. Venus in the 12th House is bi-trine to Neptune in the 4th House and Saturn in the 8th suggests that he was sensitive to other people's needs and always ready to offer assistance. Analogously, Uranus in the 2nd House is bi-sextile to Neptune and Venus in the 4th and 12th Houses respectively revealing the talents that he hadn't uncovered. The Sun in Taurus—Moon in Leo sign polarity shows his great tendency to exaggerate and his interest in speculation while the Sun in the 12th—Moon in the 3rd House polarity shows that his desire to succeed was motivated by his need to improve his self-image. The Sun sesquiquadrate Jupiter indicates too much reliance on luck but the Moon trine Jupiter shows his optimism, good health and good opportunities. The strong bi-quincunx position of the Moon with respect to the Saturn/Pluto conjunction shows his defensive response when others showed an interest in him. The Morin Point in the 2nd Gemini decanate reveals his able mentality, his adaptability together with his love of knowledge and his artistic talent. Mercury, the ruling planet in Taurus in the 1st House, shows his attraction for mental occupations, his smooth speech and his interest in practical and pleasant things. The strong trine to Pluto shows that his mind threw off worries easily. The sub-ruler, Venus in Taurus in the 12th House, shows that he would be steadfast in love but possessive. The strong quintile of Venus to Mars indicates a strengthened ability to love.

Character Portrait

General: Independence, originality and even eccentricity were Edward's outstanding characteristics. Forceful, interesting, dramatic, rebellious and determined he conduced to results through sheer, scintillating bigness of personality and belief in himself. He enjoyed creativity in art, in the theatre and in any prominent way. He also enjoyed games and happy occupations but these may have become unsatisfactory. His personality was far too active for his individuality but his emotional and devotional nature was stimulated, giving active speech, a restless nature and a constant yearning for the unattainable. There was a great tendency to exaggerate, to express keen likes and dislikes, or to go to extremes and to be very easily influenced in all matters connected with speculation, probably towards gambling in which he placed too much reliance on luck and to sensational pleasures. However, "Clouds of Glory" were more to be expected than any self-delusion. Care would have been necessary too, to avoid over-indulgence, especially in his appetites, which could have become abnormal unless checked. Although showy, ambitious, exaggerative and extravagant, he had a changeable, optimistic, companionable and kind nature.

In general, Edward was a quick worker accomplishing much in a short time. He was fond of travelling, exploring, new scenes, thoughts and ideas. Thus he found success in foreign affairs and in religious matters.

As Edward's imagination was very vivid, music, dancing, poetry and painting were necessities of life bringing happiness and benefit. He had a good singing voice, some real poetic ability, was happy as a host and inclined to good living. On the other hand he was also happy in a quiet, secluded place as well as sometimes enjoying secret happiness. The undercurrent of his life tended to be enduringly smooth.

Negative descriptions of Edward include: avaricious, harsh, brutal, tenacious and taciturn; qualities that he may well have shown at times.

Mentality: Edward was quick-witted and mentally able seeking knowledge wherever it may have been found. Both literature and science would have been equally attractive. Mental occupations and diversions, intellectual interests and new, unusual theories would have appealed to him. Being more objective than subjective, he tended towards originality and to scientific thought. His balanced and high intellectual standard (even genius) was coupled with refined tastes and clear discrimination. His mind did not wander but concentrated, deliberated, ordered and controlled in practical, cautious and methodical ways.

Egotistical and conceited, Edward's mind would have been directed towards himself. Speech, thought, gesture and movement would have been slow and smooth. His mind may not have been that resilient but would have been directed towards practical and pleasant things. He had a tendency towards charming speech and a pleasant manner.

Edward also had some psychic gifts such as inspirational speaking, clairvoyance, the ability to prophesy as well as being able to bring his dreams back into his brain. Perception and foresight were blended with reason and intuition. He enjoyed mystery and hidden matters. In general his ideas and hunches should have been acted on. Although seemingly light, he was able to know the essence of something without having to spend much time on it. He tended not to absorb ideas but learnt by experience. He liked to think for himself and particularly later, didn't wish to be bound by conventional thought. His profound religious ideas rarely conformed with the conventions and practices of any group, sect or church. Thus he had to live by his own knowing and had to learn to value that which he understood within himself rather than use the values of others against his own ideas. He couldn't quite put his finger on all he knew about life. Answers flew by as he tried to read others' thoughts to try to understand his own truths. However, when developed, he truly became a great teacher to all sincere truth seekers.

At times, he had a tendency towards woolly thinking, indiscretion, imprudence and poor judgement. His lack of concentration (possibly involving a health issue) made it difficult for him to focus on an objective. He could become suspicious, foolhardy and defiant. However, his mind threw off worries easily and began new thought with good results in the relief of nervous tension.

Lifestyle: There were highly individual or purposeful emphases in Edward's life, in which his temperament jutted out into experience according to his own very special tastes. These tastes were particular yet also impersonal. He had robust resistance to pigeon-holing either in the neat compartments of his own nature or in the idea pockets of his associates. Hence he could not be limited to any single, steady point of application and so displayed an awkward certainty to every approach he made to his life's problems. He tried to adjust to problems and to by-pass them though rarely without nervous stress. He had a tendency to be overly-impressed with his competitors' qualifications so he was less forceful than he should have been in asserting himself and his talents.

Edward was very fond of pleasure and society. He was self-confident, full of show and so might have been popular, or to have cut something of a figure socially. He found it very difficult to settle down. The habits he had developed were not easy to change and he himself felt that there was no need to change so long as he was moderately successful doing things as he always had. He tended to live for every moment and hated making plans for the future because that limited his possibilities. He was attracted to a thousand things at the same time yet tried to understand each one in a way that would not have closed him off from any of the others. He tended to act at all times under a consideration of opposing views but was capable of unique achievement through a development of unsuspected relations in life. Although he was apt to waste his energies through his improper alignment with various situations and because he tended to be indecisive, yet his final choices were well-considered. He would have argued more for the sake of upholding an apparently true or universal principle rather than from his own need to win. In this way he could have become overly righteous. With all his knowledge he had a habit of justifying this righteousness making it difficult for him to take the advice of others.

Edward's moral nature might have become strengthened considerably towards the close of his life, but the early part was one in which psychic tendencies, or sensations, played a very important role. Unsurprisingly, he tended to give impractical but sympathetic and intuitive monetary support to artistic and charitable causes.

Relationships

Others: Edward learnt from every person he met and he impressed them as well. There was the tendency that his best opportunities came from appreciating and learning from other people's opinions. However, he had a love of freedom and a hatred of interference that may have extended to a headstrong disregard for the feelings of others. Yet he was sensitive to other people's needs and was always ready to offer assistance, which meant that some people would try to take advantage of his generosity. Many of those he served may have taken him for granted, knowing that he was always available when they needed him. Others would have sought his guidance as they strove for a life filled with worthwhile human values. Thus there was responsibility through the affairs of others, either through financial cares, or through losses caused by them. He tried to avoid being obliged to others, perhaps by trying to advance himself by ruthless behaviour towards them, although his circumstances indicated that he couldn't really escape it.

Edward looked at himself as seen through the eyes of others. There was an impatient tendency to try to please others, although he was not sure what prompted this. He constantly ran into people whose philosophical attitudes towards life ran contrary to his own and he tended to place too much emphasis on the ideas that others presented to him. He came to learn that differences between right and wrong existed strictly in the mind of the observer. He came to see how fruitless it was for him to make decisions or value judgements for other people. Simultaneously, on many different levels, he was learning to balance the nature of truth through the many ways it was expressed from person to person in his life.

Friends: Edward sought the company of strong characters who weren't slaves to materialism for he was impressed by those who had strong religious convictions and whose ethical standards were not easily swayed. He could have spread himself too thinly by trying to gain the respect of those he admired and yet with all these efforts he knew that he would still be unable to please the entire world.

Edward might have been surprised to learn that many of his friends and acquaintances admired him for his knowledge and for his readiness to help those in need. He was overly demonstrative in expressing his fondness for his close friends and they may have taken advantage of his kindness. He always found time to do favours for his friends and he didn't even consider it an intrusion on his freedom. However, he received unfavourable responses to support given to wide-ranging friends. He should have been at least as attentive to his future financial security as he was to his friends.

Family: Although Edward's relations with his mother had not been easy, he experienced happiness himself through his own children.

Having children brought out the best in him. However, he showed eccentricity in ways of taking care of anyone or anything resulting in an uneasy expression of affection and in a lack of harmony in the home. Yet his family was very important to him and he was worrying constantly about whether they had everything they needed even though fulfilling his obligations to his family may have proved irritating if it kept him from indulging his personal interests. In reality, he should have directed some of his efforts to developing new skills that he could have used when his family no longer required his attention. Still, his children considered him exciting and they admired his many talents.

Lover: Once freed to seek his own destiny Edward may well have turned his attention to satisfying his personal desires in a relationship. Although there was happiness and success through love affairs, Edward was inconstant, being all talk rather than having any real feeling for someone else. His relationships with women were not easy and so his affections might have been drawn easily into unfortunate channels, but his romantic partners stayed interested because they never knew what to expect from him. Unusualness was apt to be fascinating and compulsive but perhaps also somewhat unpleasant. He became capable of keeping his love affairs secret. His partnerships were unconventional and apt to be broken because of his insistence on freedom. In addition there was a tenseness that was hard to relax and which caused nerve storms. Because he was unwilling to see anyone's negative qualities, he was extremely vulnerable in his love affairs. He needed to question and to examine closely every important contact he made. As a result partings were likely through unhappy causes. Unfortunately his affections and relationships were subject to disclosures, upheavals and new starts—some with trouble and unpleasantness but others with good results in the end. His ensuing sense of lack intensified his shyness and prevented an easy response to what could have brought happiness. He became somewhat defensive when others showed an interest in him because he questioned their motives. He was unsure whether their interest was physical or intellectual. He needed to give people a chance before he jumped to conclusions. This limitation of affection, or of a happy social life, could have had its reward in a serious, single direction. Love may have meant sacrifice, or a life lonely, except for the chosen one.

Edward developed fairly good judgement in handling relationships but he hated to make hasty decisions. He was steadfast in love but possessive. Although he was slow to make serious partnerships (with impecunious partners?) he was reliable and successful in a practical way once settled.

Edward's lower nature was ardent and, at times, passionate. His ability to love and to enjoy sexual life was strengthened, made more robust, but less delicate. At a higher level, Edward's sexual drive was lowered so tending to put his relationships on a more superficial level. He preferred a relationship in which he could satisfy his physical needs without undue pressure. However, unless he knew that he was satisfying his partner's need for companionship as well as for his/her physical requirements, then he would have lost interest. He wanted to be a good companion as well as a lover to his partner but he was turned off by any pressure to commit himself to a binding alliance.

Edward's fate was affected by marriage, or love affairs, yet he wasn't inclined towards marriage and preferred a celibate life. If married, he would have been attracted to a partner, who may well have been overly righteous. In any case marriage and partnerships would have played a major role in his life and may well have brought about a rise in his social status coupled with significant material benefits. Edward worked hard to earn the respect and admiration of his partner, for he thought that s/he would accept him only if he provided all of life's necessities. He accepted this requirement but he didn't extend himself generally, beyond the essentials, if he could have avoided it. Edward would have devoted himself to a partner who appreciated him and supported him in his endeavours. In fact, a close love relationship would have given him the impetus to assert himself in his career. It would have been ideal if his mate had shared his life's focus, sympathised with his objectives and had worked with him to achieve them. A partner who understood his hang-ups and who believed in his abilities would have worked wonders for his self-esteem. His partner should have known when to get involved with his pursuits and when to let him be by himself. If someone he loved and respected had a strong belief in his abilities he would have listened to him/her.

Career

Early: Edward's destiny lay mainly in his own hands and he knew it. He had a tendency to a lucky journey through life, during which he met good opportunities and helpful people. Often his fate was affected by relatives, by his companions and by his philosophical attitude, which decided whether he became a mere imitator or copier of others, or one who awakened his own spiritual tendencies that were latent within.

Edward may not have enjoyed the arduous task of getting an education and he certainly hated to give up his own free time spent on self-indulgence but he knew that without an education he would have been limited. His favourable early conditioning had allowed him to make his own way without restrictions. Luckily his parents probably understood his need to conduct his affairs in his own way but this early conditioning was also the main cause of his unwillingness to deal with his responsibility to develop his creativity so that he could succeed. He might have assumed that he had to have his parents' approval before taking action, so he lost interest. In practice, he should have been allowed to make decisions and to fail in them if necessary, so that he didn't make the same mistake again. Unless he had been free and independent, he would never have known the joy of success. He wanted so much to know that he was making an important contribution to improve conditions for others. Primarily he wanted to succeed in realising his ambitions to improve his self-image because he was filled with uncertainty and apprehension about his abilities. Secretly he feared that he wouldn't really measure up to people's expectations. The fact was that, generally, he proved himself beyond anyone's expectations. He tried to convince himself that he had the qualifications to reach his goals but, at the same time, he found it difficult to define exactly what he wanted. Many people have had the same anxieties but have been motivated to overcome them.

Edward had talents that he hadn't uncovered, but his was the responsibility for developing them. He was more resourceful and qualified than he knew. He had to find a career that made demands on him and which forced him to use his natural talent. If he had done this he would have been well-paid. He could have developed his artistic talent if he had been honest with himself and admitted that he had creativity. He was clever and inventive in ideas to aid work, especially of the designing, craftsmanship or scientific type. This untapped potential could have increased his wealth and freedom.

Edward's success in striving for significance depended on how well he used his creativity. Self-development was the key. He could have become a credit to himself by building a sound mind in a sound body. He had to have found a way to make a meaningful contribution to society either through personal or group activities. With his knowledge and readiness to help others he could have chosen a career that would have brought success and would have satisfied his need to do something constructive. His talent for improving existing social conditions was much needed. Working behind the scenes for some worthwhile activity may have been necessary and would have proved an enriching experience. Working with young people may have given him much satisfaction, for he could have helped them to stand on their own. Providing a service that improved the quality of life for large numbers of people was also consistent with his temperament. Industry would have had many uses for his skills and any business would have been helped by his insights about how to meet the public's expectations. His creativity and his ability to communicate could have formed the basis for a career in writing, reporting, broadcasting, psychological counselling, medical research or education.

Middle: Edward was subject to upsets and to forced new phases. He over valued the practical and he had a tendency to meet hardships. He compared his resources with those of others as though he thought his self-worth should have been determined only by his personal and material assets.

Edward did have an ability to adapt to circumstances—good or bad—that would have persisted throughout his life. However, unless he was actually willing to adapt to changing circumstances, his ability to succeed was limited. He mustn't have been afraid to look ahead to see what was coming, so that when conditions did change, he was still in demand. He was qualified to carry out the research and development that had to take place before changes could have been accepted. If he had helped to make the changes, he could have been ready when they occurred.

Although Edward may have been restricted by the demanding obligations of his daily routine, he managed to use his innovative ability to make his work interesting. However, he hated the confinement of a daily routine because it limited his freedom but he wouldn't really be free until he had applied himself and earned it. Still, he was clever at devising new and better ways to make his tasks more exciting. Basically he became confident of his ability, and was imaginative enough, to make a worthwhile life for himself once he had established a solid foundation. Then all he needed was the opportunity to grow as his needs dictated.

Edward undertook a serious and vital search for the meaning of life. He was in touch with the pulse of social evolution. He could have played an important role in determining the quality of society by his personal commitment to the highest and most spiritual behaviour. He was preoccupied with gaining freedom from want, which was precious to him. He had a strong compulsion to make his services available at the social level of human need as his contribution to the welfare of society and so would have liked to use his talents to help those who were unable to help themselves. He held strong opinions about social conditions that needed to be changed but if he had wanted to derive any benefit from his ideas, then he must have accepted the burden of developing and implementing them at the social level. This sensitivity to unacceptable social conditions may have forced him to make some sacrifices to ensure the elimination of these conditions. Generally, he expressed the need for support, help and charity well during his career. Usually he achieved his goals by implementing his ideas successfully without arousing the anxieties of those who worked with him. He communicated best through his efforts at the task and he cultivated the best public relations by working hard for those who had requested his services. Constantly he had to call upon his wealth of ideas so that they could have benefitted himself and others. He was always looking for better ways to use his creativity and secretly planned how to promote his ideas for the greatest gain. His ability to present his ideas convincingly to interested persons who had the financial resources to back them was one of his strong points. Thus his ideas attracted attention and gave him what he needed to realise his goals.

<u>Late:</u> Edward had more need for security than it seemed because he often tended to fail to plan ahead for it and because he was so

fascinated with the present. He had to learn to continue working to serve the needs of others. This was how he could have made his best contribution and have gained financial security for his later years. He hoped to retire early enough to enjoy the benefits of his productive years and indulge himself without worrying about money. He may have said that he couldn't wait to retire but when the time came he may have resisted it because he enjoyed being involved with the world. He didn't need to have worried about filling his leisure time because he had a rich variety of outside interests.

Appearance and Health

Appearance: Edward had a tall, slender and erect figure that was strong and well-formed, with a square build later due to becoming stout. His face would have been long but also fleshy. His complexion was sanguine but good. Probably he had hazel eyes and possibly he was good-looking.

Health: Edward had a strong constitution and sound, good health. There were no neuroses through the suppression of his unconscious self. Changes, new ideas and "differentness" were applied to food and precautions about health. There may have been some trouble from the incorrect working of his liver with his nervous system that may have led to woolly thinking, indiscretion and poor judgement.

Possibly his death may have occurred unfortunately in a public place but there was also an indication of the possibility of death in his old age following from a chronic complaint or from the results of a long-standing accident or from unusual diseases.

- -

Reference: 'Edward II', Seymour Phillips, Yale University Press Publications, New Haven, U.S.A., and London, U.K., 2010.

- -

EDWARD III

"Let the boy earn his spurs."
Speaking about his eldest son, Edward, The Black Prince,
at the battle of Crécy, 1346.

Edward was one of the most successful monarchs of the Middle Ages. Restoring royal authority after the disastrous reign of his father, Edward II, he went on to transform England into the most efficient military power in Europe. Edward's reign saw vital developments in legislature, government and especially the evolution of the English parliament. The ravages of the Black Death occurred during his reign, which lasted for fifty years.

Edward was crowned at the age of fourteen following his father's abdication. At age seventeen he led a coup against his regent, Roger Mortimer. After defeating, but not subjugating, Scotland, he declared himself the rightful heir to the French throne in 1340, thereby starting the Hundred Years' War. After some initial setbacks, the war went exceptionally well for England; the victories of Sluys, Crécy, Poitiers and the capture of Calais, led to the highly favourable Treaty of Brétigny. However, Edward's later years were marked by international failure and domestic strife due largely to his inertia and eventual bad health.

Edward was a temperamental man but also capable of great clemency. He was mostly conventional, mainly interested in warfare and became highly revered in his own time and later. Although denounced earlier, modern biographers credit him with remarkable achievements.

Figure 13: King Edward III's Epoch Chart

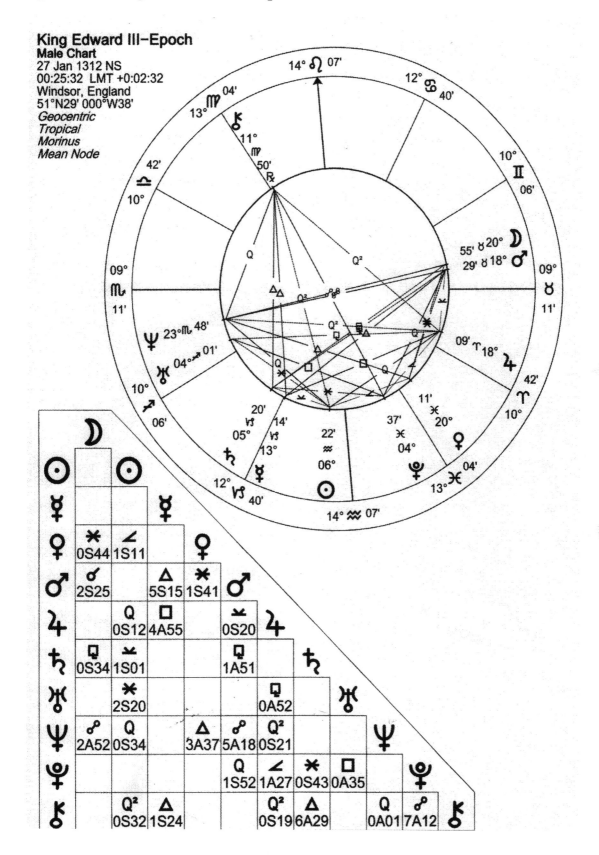

King Edward III–Epoch
Male Chart
27 Jan 1312 NS
00:25:32 LMT +0:02:32
Windsor, England
51°N29' 000°W38'
Geocentric
Tropical
Morinus
Mean Node

Edward was the first child and son of King Edward II of England and Queen Isabella of France. He was born on the 21st November, 1312 NS at 05:30, at Windsor, England (see Figure 14). His Epoch occurred on the 27th January, 1312 NS, at 00:25 (see Figure 13). We see that, at Epoch, the planets lie mainly below the Earth (North) indicating his subjective nature and that the overall shaping is a 'Bucket' with Chiron in Virgo in the 11th House as the slightly anti-clockwise handle planet across the Neptune opposition to the Moon/Mars conjunction as the rim of the bucket. This suggests that he gave and received practical and critical support from his friends. The bucket shaping suggests a particular and uncompromising direction to his life effort. The Sun in Aquarius—Moon in Taurus sign polarity shows true insight into human nature and that he should take stock before marrying too soon, while the Sun in 4th—Moon in 7th House polarity shows his strong family ties but also his need to become involved with other people in society. The Sun quintile Jupiter shows cheerfulness, contentedness, helpful people, good opportunities and luck. The Moon conjoint Mars in Taurus in the 7th House indicates a robust, courageous nature and the combined opposition to Neptune indicates sensitivity but also a tendency towards reserve. The Morin Point in Scorpio could show a potentially criminal personality but also the possibility for success by means of prudence, dignity and a thrusting, purposeful and hard working nature. Pluto (the ruler) in Pisces in the 5th House, square Uranus and sextile to Saturn indicates compassion, imagination, fluctuating resources and that renunciation, in general, could well become an obsession.

Figure 14: King Edward III's Birth Chart.

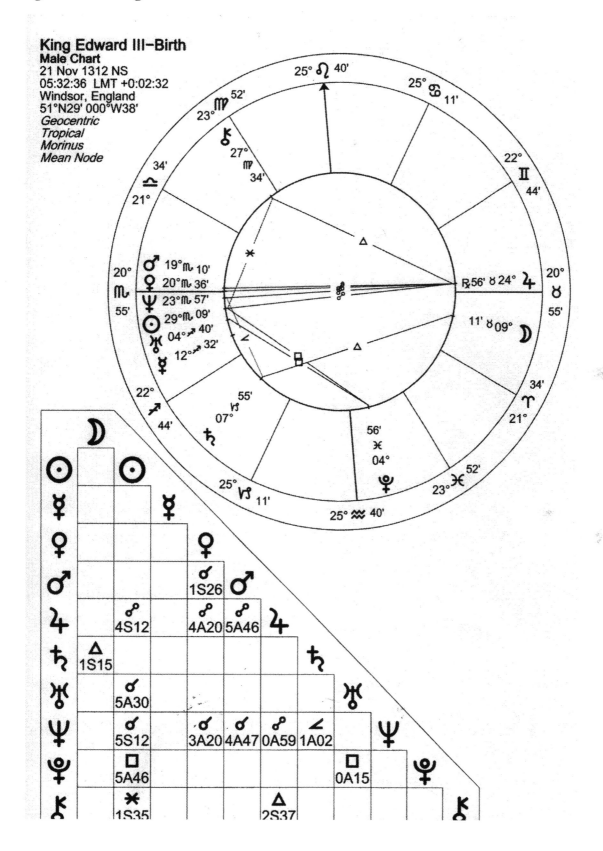

King Edward III—Birth
Male Chart
21 Nov 1312 NS
05:32:36 LMT +0:02:32
Windsor, England
51°N29' 000°W38'
Geocentric
Tropical
Morinus
Mean Node

Notice that the Epoch chart contains seven quintile family aspects that impart intelligence to Edward's character.

The Epoch chart generates the Ideal Birth Chart (see Figure 14). Here the planets lie mainly to the East showing that Edward's destiny lay mostly in his own hands. The overall shaping of the chart is a fanhandle of which Jupiter is the focal planet, retrograde in Taurus in the 7th House. This means that it would have been difficult for Edward to adapt himself to other people's way of thinking. It suggests also that he was able to see himself easily through the eyes of others. The opposition of Jupiter to Neptune suggests treachery but that this could be mitigated by the trine to Chiron and the sextile of Chiron to Neptune, i.e. by good support from friends. The Sun in Scorpio—Moon in Taurus sign polarity reveals his love of display and the Sun in 1st—Moon in 7th House polarity shows how well he responded to challenges. The Morin Point in the 3rd Scorpio decanate shows his desire for attachment and the attendant jealous tendencies. Pluto (the ruler) in Pisces in the 4th House, square to Uranus, reveals the vital part played by his negative and upsetting parental influence that forced him to exert himself and to succeed on his own. Notice that Mercury in Sagittarius in the 2nd House is unaspected. This means that his mentality was not well-integrated with the rest of his personality. In this case his 'far-flung' ideas about his resources may have had little to do with his overall nature. Venus, Mars and Neptune, all in conjunction, and all rising in Scorpio suggests that his greatest danger was being deceived by others, that his ability to love and enjoy sexual life was strengthened, that he lacked an ability to be happy alone and that he liked to be 'spoilt' plus much amusing social life. Notice, finally, that the Morin Point for both Edward's charts lies in Scorpio. Additionally the position of the Moon in both charts lies in Taurus. This unusual, combined situation simplifies interpretation but also emphasises the importance of these two major indicators in his charts.

Character Portrait

General: Edward was generally fortunate, cheerful and contented with his own surroundings. Faithful, reliable, firm, determined, genial, warm, affectionate and even genteel, he liked to be 'spoilt' and became very fond of amusing social life. Thus his robust and courageous manner was softened with increased display but his emotions and desires were deep and strong so that, at times, he was over-active and overly quick to respond. Being subjective, music, art and all matters about the sea were cultivated. Although he had enhanced sensitivity, there was also the possibility for treachery, deceit and gullibility. On the more negative side, he could be self-willed, fanatical, rash and boastful.

Mentality: Edward was intelligent and prudent but dogmatically tended to hold on stubbornly to past concepts. Although his ideas and hunches came easily, he spent too much time living in the clouds.

He spent much energy establishing that he was always right but this made it difficult for him to adapt himself to other people's way of thinking. However, he would argue to uphold a principle rather than from his own need to win. As a result, he could become overly self-righteous and quarrelsome and so needed to learn that differences between right and wrong lay strictly in the mind of each individual. He was learning to balance the nature of truth through the many ways it was expressed from person to person in his life. Actually, his mentality was not well-integrated with the rest of his personality. Thus, thoughts expressed in 'far-flung', decisive, money-making ways were not necessarily part of his true character and so needed to be guarded against.

Lifestyle: Edward's desire to enlarge the scope of his personal expression would have been strong, forceful and perhaps overdone.

He was restless, eager and, when stimulated, his aggressive nature sprang into action. It was the thrill of competition that made him accept challenges. Challenge was the most stimulating situation for him and literally he glowed as he rose to the occasion. He thrived on sensationalism and conflict. Even when situations became bogged down and he became bored and lost interest, he thrived on the many confrontations that he faced. As a result, Edward had no desire to conserve either himself or his resources. He dipped deeply into life and poured forth the result of his gathered experiences with unremitting zeal. However, in reality, he had a fixed course of life and persisted and persevered to carry it out. In fact, he lived in a groove all his life. Mostly, he needed to feel dominant but actually learnt his greatest truths when he was not trying to impress others or when not trying to exert himself.

At his worst, Edward had a criminal personality seeking fulfilment of personal aims without regard for the feelings of others. However, if he could have resisted these tendencies, then honest success could have been achieved by means of a thrusting, purposeful nature and a capacity for hard work. Fortunately, his compassion and imagination were stimulated. Later on, renunciation may well have become an obsession with him and probably he developed a compelling need to achieve understanding.

Relationships

<u>Others:</u> Edward looked at himself as seen through the eyes of others. He even experienced impatience trying to please others. He taught himself to stand for what he thought others would admire. Put simply, he wanted people to like him. He always tried to be pleasant because he truly enjoyed people and he won the approval of those around him by conceding to their desires if he could. He was an instructor and inspirer of others. Yet it disturbed him to be ignored as he was

much more sensitive than others realised. Additionally, his relations with women were not easy but, generally, his social side became well-developed with good public relations and the meeting of helpful people. Basically, he could not function well unless he was involved with people and indeed most of his opportunities came from the social contacts he made. He was completely involved with the world around him. Nevertheless, he wasn't sure that he could live up to others' expectations of him. If necessary, either he would flatter people when he wanted to win them over or, he made certain concessions to win their support in his climb to prominence. His ability to perform would have been increased if he could have avoided getting too involved with the people he dealt with.

His greatest danger was being deceived by others. He should have had to check everyone's credentials and he had to believe only the facts that checked out. He should have had legal advice even for insignificant contracts. Yet he could read character and he was immediately aware when anyone tried to undermine him or resorted to unfair practices.

Friends: Edward was good with friends and acquaintances winning them over by using his charm. There was never a dull moment when he was around because he lent sparkle and wit to any gathering. He was well-liked by his friends because he didn't threaten their egos. However, in general, he waited for the other person to make the first approach because he feared rejection or a lack of interest. Thus, his need for companionship meant that he had to make many concessions to others. Although not perfect himself, he had a somewhat conservative, wounded healer approach for supporting and helping friends, who tended to be both practical and critical when receiving or reciprocating favours in turn.

<u>Family:</u> Frequent changes of Edward's home were likely and there may have been a tendency for him to adopt an unconventional way of life. Alienating circumstances at home would have forced him to assert himself and feel confident so that he would have been able to succeed on his own when the time came. His relationship with his mother may not have been easy and he had a vital and deeply-upsetting parental influence during which his father died when young. Even so, his strong family ties made it difficult for him to transfer his attention to other people in society. Hence his first task was to become more detached from his family, putting them in the proper perspective that allowed him the independence to come and go as the demands of his career and social life required.

Edward's domestic side was well-developed. Probably he would have enjoyed indulging his children as he had a strong mothering tendency always in the background of his consciousness and this might have helped to satisfy his hunger for attention. As a result, he had difficulty gaining the independence he needed from family obligations but he used his charm to smooth over any domestic disagreements.

<u>Lover:</u> Edward's ability to love, to enjoy sexual life and all things of beauty was strengthened and made more robust but less delicate. He was passionate, intense, sensual and secretive in love but his easy charm and desire for partnership was overdone. He had a lack of ability to be happy alone and a keen desire for attachment that tended to counter selfishness but jealous tendencies could have been exacerbated. He would have been willing to make sacrifices for the 'right' person, with whom he wanted to share his life, and no gift would have been too costly when he wanted to impress that person. However, he needed to resist the urge to marry the first likely prospect. His early training had led him to believe that it was better to marry anyone than to remain single. With that attitude he

could have ended up being single again. He should have postponed marrying until he was sure that he wasn't trying to compensate for a poor parental image in his choice of partner for such a situation is rarely satisfying. But he needed to be involved in a partnership and marriage would have been an asset to him in his future plans. Yet his partnership may not have been what it seemed and he may not have been so fortunate in marriage. His mate must have been willing to share his enthusiasm for what he hoped to accomplish, which would have improved the quality of life for his family. If someone he loved and respected had a strong belief in his abilities he would have listened to her/him.

Career

Early: Edward's destiny was in his own hands and he would have been fairly fortunate through life, during which opportunities and good luck would have been expected. His parents taught him to take advantage of every opportunity to further his growth and development. His optimism grew from their belief that he could succeed if he wanted to. Education supported his purposes leading to involvement with large numbers of people from a position of authority. He came to learn that careful planning was the best way to achieve his goals. It would have been through his response to challenges and competition presented by others that he proved himself eventually. His ultimate ambition was to gain full control over his circumstances. Restless in his birthplace he had an over-exaggerated desire to aggrandise himself through more land and what this could achieve.

Middle: Edward inherited great transformations which he realised through self-determination and the leverage of power. The whole world was his home, he knew what he wanted and he knew how to get it. There was an uncompromising direction to his life effort and he adapted his allegiances to lines along which he could make his efforts count for the most. His frame of reference had to become increasingly intellectual, not emotional, to improve his ability to solve the many problems that he met. Being emotionally committed in his duties would have severely limited his effectiveness. It annoyed him to be without money but he had no excuse because his creativity should have allowed him to increase his resources. He expected more from his efforts than he deserved because he didn't want to give up his indulgences. He should have applied himself.

Edward would have been interested in occupations that brought him before the public. He was concerned about social problems and had many ideas to solve them. His sensitive understanding of human problems proved an asset for public service but he had to be careful not to allow people to use him as a doormat. He showed a willing acceptance of duty and gained success through orderly and practical ways even though these may have caused personal limitations and a lack of gaiety. He was often overly impressed by his competitors' qualifications, because he was less forceful than he should have been in asserting himself and his talent. Work was plentiful, lucrative and contacts with workers were usually cheerful and good but there may have been some poor management relations.

<u>Later:</u> Edward looked forward to the time when he could feel free from daily harassment and effort. By using all his resources he could easily have achieved this goal.

Health

<u>Appearance:</u> Edward was of middle stature, stout, well-made and physically strong. He had a full, swarthy, fleshy face with dark grey eyes, prominent brows, an aquiline nose and profile, and dark brown hair.

<u>Health:</u> He had good health but there was a tendency towards nervous disorders that perhaps were aggravated by inner struggles. Also there was the possibility for paralysis (brought on by strokes?) and for accidents. Isolated circumstances were indicated for him at the end of his life.

Reference: "The Perfect King—The Life of Edward III, Father of the English Nation", Ian Mortimer, Pimlico, Random House Group, London, 2007.

RICHARD II

"What a strange land this is, and a fickle, which has exiled, slain, destroyed or ruined so many kings, rulers and great men, and is ever tainted with strife and envy."

Richard succeeded to the throne in 1377 at the age of ten following the death of his grandfather, Edward III. During his first years as king government was in the hands of a series of councils. The political community preferred this to a regency led by Richard's uncle, John of Gaunt, who nevertheless remained highly influential. The Peasants' Revolt in 1381 provided the first major challenge to his reign, which the young king handled well. Subsequently, Richard's dependence on a small number of courtiers caused political discontent and in 1387 control of government was taken over by a group of noblemen known as the Lords Appellant. Richard regained control in 1389 and governed with his opponents for the next eight years. Then, in 1397, he took his revenge and had many of them executed. In 1399, after John of Gaunt died, Richard disinherited his son, Henry, who previously had been exiled. Henry invaded England later in 1399 with a small force that quickly grew in numbers, meeting little resistance. Henry deposed Richard and had himself crowned Henry IV. Richard died in captivity early the next year; he might well have been murdered (but see Health).

As an individual Richard was said to have been tall and intelligent. Less of a warrior than either his father or grandfather, he sought to bring an end to the Hundred Years' War that Edward III had started. Again, by contrast with the fraternal, martial court of the latter, Richard cultivated a courtly atmosphere with himself at the head and art and culture at the centre. He was a firm believer in the royal prerogative, which led him to restrain the power of his nobility and rely on a private retinue for military protection instead. Even though Richard's policies were with precedent and perhaps realistic, the way in which he tried to implement them was unacceptable to the political community, which, in turn, led to his downfall.

- -

Richard was the younger and only surviving son of Edward, the Black Prince and of Joan, the Maid of Kent. His parents were 2nd cousins once removed having King Edward I as their common paternal great grandfather but the Black Prince's paternal great grandmother was Eleanor of Castile, whereas his mother Joan's was Margaret of France. Hence, they were not 2nd cousins in the usual way but still they had needed a special dispensation from the Pope in order to marry.

Richard was born on the 14th January, 1367 NS at 10:10 at Bordeaux, France (see Figure 16). His Epoch occurred on 3rd April, 1366 NS at 05:09 (see Figure 15). Examination of his Epoch chart shows that his planets lie mainly in the North East quadrant suggesting that his destiny lay mainly in his own hands and that he was subjective. The overall planetary shaping is 'See-Saw' meaning that he acted at all times under a consideration of opposing views that tended to produce indecision but that his final choices would have been well-considered. Mercury retrograde in Aries in the 2nd House is the focal point of a Yod to the Moon and Jupiter. This indicates that he wanted financial independence but also that he wanted to be well-thought of. The opposition of the Moon to Neptune is mediated favourably by Jupiter showing sensitivity but also a tendency to retirement, philanthropy, day-dreaming and escapism. The Sun in Aries—Moon in Virgo sign polarity reveals a critical and discriminatory tendency stimulated by practical and scie-

Figure 15: King Richard II's Epoch Chart.

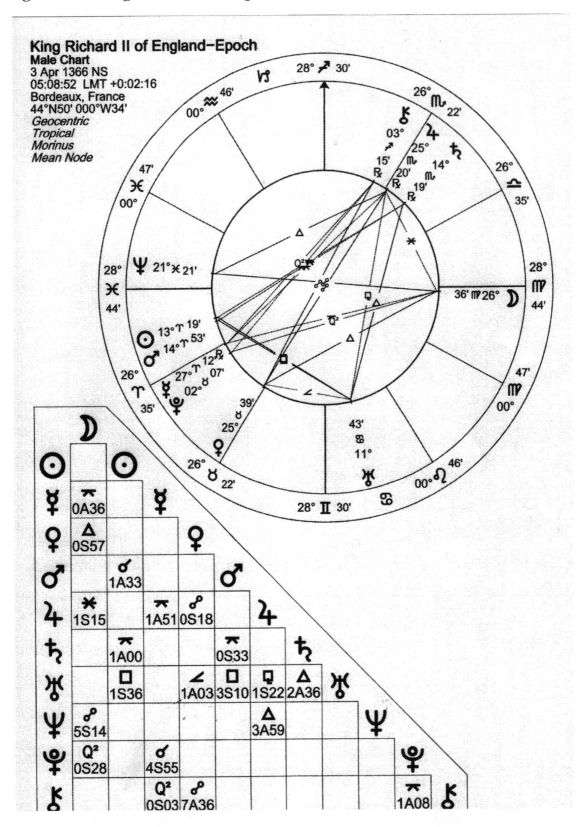

ntific traits. The Sun in the 2nd—Moon in 7th House polarity suggests that he did not function at his best unless he was involved in some kind of relationship. The Sun conjoint Mars shows that he expressed himself energetically. In the 2nd House this suggests that security was his most important consideration. The Moon trine Venus indicates a love of beauty, interest in the arts and a good, balanced outlook. The Moon biquintile Pluto (the sub-ruler) shows that even violent, changeful happenings could have been turned to good account. The Moon sextile Jupiter indicates optimism, good health and a tendency to a lucky journey through life. The Morin Point in the 3rd Pisces decanate reveals a strongly artistic personality. Neptune (the ruler) rising in Pisces shows sympathy, some crazy notions and a philanthropic outlook, whereas Pluto (the sub-ruler) in Taurus in the 2nd House indicates an obsession with wealth and a compelling need to achieve permanence. Mercury retrograde in Aries in the 2nd House shows that impatience in his thought processes often led to poor judgement.

The Epoch generates the Birth chart shown in Figure 16. Notice that both charts contain only four quintile family aspects to support intelligence but that imagination and scientific indicators support an intelligence interpretation (by contrast his father's combined natal charts show nine quintile family aspects). Notice also that both Richard's natal charts have the Morin Point in the 3rd Pisces decanate. This is because the Moon at birth is rising here making the Morin Point at Epoch, in this case, occupy the same position. This unusual situation is reminiscent of Richard's grandfather's (Edward III's) natal charts in which the Morin Point in both cases occurred in Scorpio (see Figures 13 and 14). This simplifies interpretation but it does emphasise the importance of the major, Morin Point indicator in their respective charts. Additionally, Edward I himself had his Morin Point at birth in the 3rd Pisces decanate, with Jupiter (and Chiron) ris-

Figure 16: King Richard II's Birth Chart.

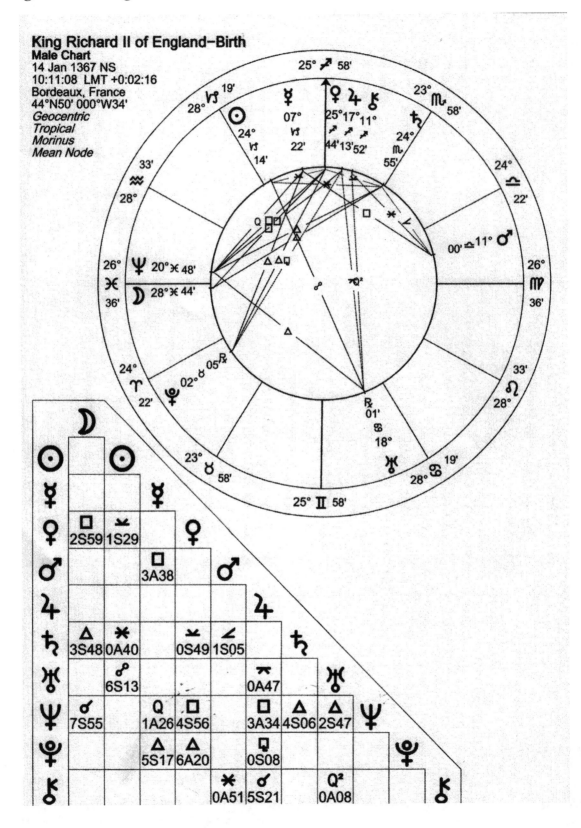

ing in his case (see Figure 10). For completeness, we also recall that Neptune (the ruler) was rising close to the Morin Point in the 3ʳᵈ Pisces decanate for King Henry III's speculative Birth chart (see Figure 8).

Richard's Birth chart shows that the planets lie mainly to the South suggesting objectivity. The overall chart shaping is a distorted 'Bucket' with Uranus as the perpendicular, handle planet. However, there is no clearly defined opposition to mark out the bucket's rim. Nevertheless Uranus is clearly a focal planet in the chart indicating that, at a higher level, he would have been in tune with the then new developments in civilisation. The bucket shaping itself suggests a particular and uncompromising direction to his life effort. We notice that Neptune (the ruler) rising is bi-trine to Saturn and Uranus indicating remarkable inspiration but also that Richard would have been dreamy and easily influenced to submit to people and situations. Venus in Sagittarius in the 10ᵗʰ House is bi-semisextile to the Sun and Saturn showing that the worst thing he could have done was to doubt his ability to do what he wanted to do. The Sun in Capricorn and Moon in Pisces sign polarity reveals a quiet, easy-going nature while the Sun in the 11ᵗʰ—Moon in the 1ˢᵗ House polarity reveals moods fluctuating from highs to lows and so his need for understanding friends. The Sun sextile Saturn shows that he accepted what was lacking but that his wisdom would grow as the years passed. The Moon square Venus and trine Saturn implies an uneasy expression of affection but a willing acceptance of duty that could have led to success. Pluto (the sub-ruler) in Taurus in the 2ⁿᵈ House but now sesquiquadrate to Jupiter in Sagittarius in the 10ᵗʰ House indicates a compulsive desire to achieve by bursting away from existing conditions but which was likely to lead to further bondage. The Moon rising in the 3ʳᵈ Pisces decanate suggests a truly hospitable person, but more ready to suffer than to act, as well as being given to forebodings. Uranus, the focal planet, in Cancer in the 5ᵗʰ House, shows his eccentricity in taking care of anyone and with little regard for convention in love affairs.

Character Portrait

General: Richard appears to have been a mixture of strongly contrasting character traits resulting in personal confusion and distrust. On the one hand he had a strongly artistic personality with an interest in the psychic, the mystical and the occult. His mediumship was easily called upon. He showed an empathy with all things of the sea as well as a fondness for dumb animals. Quiet, mild-mannered, undemonstrative and easy-going, he was sympathetic, kind, refined, philanthropic, humane, sensitive impressionable and well-adapted to express his emotions intellectually. He loved order, poetry and idealistic conditions in general. Although he was truly hospitable and compassionate, at his worst he could have been soft, timid, yielding and passive and given to forebodings, being more ready to suffer than to act.

Yet Richard didn't show his whole nature on the surface by any means. He could, on the other hand, be bold, strong, enduring, forceful and brave as well as quick and hard-working. Thus he could also express himself energetically. Selfishness, jealousy, conventionality, dreaminess and escapism constituted negative aspects of his nature including his cultivation of the material side of life.

Mentality: Continuing with the idea of a mixture of opposing traits we can suggest that the subjective side of Richard's good, balanced mentality enabled him to be inspirational, optimistic, spiritual and in tune with the mystical. His moods of dreaminess and inattention caused him to become lost in a world of imagination and crazy notions that could have proved useful for works of art, literature and intuition in everyday and professional life. Because of his affinity for philosophical and spiritual matters he needed a formal education to develop these mental faculties further. In this way he could have become highly responsive to any new order of civilisation. However, the objective side of Richard's mentality that used his critical, accurate, discriminatory as well as practical, exacting and scientific aptitudes enabled his ideals to be carried into actuality by initiative, unusual power and advanced leadership. Despite a utilitarian outlook, he had a love of study, abilities for literature, musical expression and possibly creative brilliance. Perhaps understandably, he could, at times, have been self-willed, awkward and brusque.

Richard's thought processes could have become so deeply rooted in the practical that he had difficulty seeing the relative importance of other levels in life. Much of his attention was focused on money yet he could be penny-wise and pound-foolish. He carried with him crystallised thought, which he held onto stubbornly. He became defensive of the value systems he had worked so hard on to derive. Easily growing possessive of his past thoughts he was able to fixate himself in one obsession after another. His thought patterns reflected his almost child-like desire to prove his mental competence. Constantly wondering if he was good enough in the eyes of the world he raced forward to meet his past challenges but these were now no longer relevant. Lacking patience he often judged poorly through impulsive thinking. This tended to put him out-of-time with most people he talked to, yet he was a strong debater, enjoying the challenge of mental stimulation. This enabled him to prove himself worthy.

Richard hated repeating himself and complained actively about having to live in a world that had lost its stimulation by continually reconsidering actions that it had already completed. Yet paradoxically, he tended to repeat himself a great deal, eventually boring those around him. He would have become the happiest of people if only he had been able to transcend old, worn-out habit patterns that constantly had been pulling him down.

<u>Lifestyle:</u> Sometimes Richard was rather retiring and self-distrustful but he possessed better abilities than people supposed. However, he lacked opportunity to use them to advantage. His obsession was wealth with a compelling need to achieve permanence. Sympathetic and charitable according to his means, he possessed tact, diplomacy, secrecy and reserve. He became conditioned to what was lacking. Lessons of duty, self-control, wisdom, patience and constructiveness were learnt and grew into what could have brought success in later life. Security was his most important consideration and he put a lot of energy into acquiring the necessities of life to have an advantage over those who lacked them.

In nearly all Richard did, he was a creature of habit and he often met difficulties breaking any past behaviour patterns associated with overindulgence/abstinence (see health). Yet he liked new phases and changeful happenings in life and even though these were violent, they were turned to good account. He also had a tendency to be impractical in that he concentrated more on visions of the future rather than on those of the present. He may have been preoccupied with personal matters when he should have directed his attention to external affairs. Additionally, he tended to over-estimate his power based on his accumulated assets. Pride in personal qualifications was apt to carry him beyond the limits of the fear of consequences tending to make him hard and unfeeling.

Richard acted at all times under a consideration of opposing views, making him seem indecisive but his final choices were well-made. He had no basic desire to conserve himself or his resources and so he dipped deeply into life and poured forth the gathered result of his experiences with unremitting zeal. There was a spiritual factor underlying his eagerness to handle social responsibility. He was one of those who 'brought good tidings' and whose 'feet were beautiful on the mountains'.

Relationships

<u>Others:</u> Richard wanted helpful people and the public to think of him as a person with solid, human values. He was a real instructor and inspirer of others. He could have won the public's sympathy with his warmth and sincerity. He made a good impression on people because he showed that he was really concerned about their problems and so he could have left a lasting impression on them by his sacrifices. His ability to function socially would have been improved as he learnt to express himself more freely. Being a good listener was fine but it didn't tell people that he may have had many useful and creative ideas. He knew what people expected of him and he capitalised on this but even though he usually perceived what people really meant, he could have been misled by deliberate untruths. The tendency was that his greatest danger was being deceived by others. To try to avoid this he needed to keep as well informed as possible. He needed also to check everyone's credentials and believe only those facts that he could check. He should have had legal advice even for insignificant contracts.

Richard judged people by their physical assets, paying little attention to their human qualities yet, on the other hand, he seemed interested only in people who had substantial human values. As an idealist with a deep appreciation of philosophical and spiritual matters, he was pained to see how little was done to improve the quality of life for many people in society. He was upset by people in important positions who had distorted public values. His compassion went out to those who were sociologically and economically locked into unfortunate situations. By getting a formal education, he could have given his professional attention to those social conditions. However, he was very sensitive and easily influenced to submit to people and situations. His insecurity made others apprehensive about dealing with him. To avoid unpleasantness he often withdrew when he should have been more aggressive. If he had have been motivated to do whatever he wanted with his power, people were likely to have resented him. Consequently, he may have suffered seriously through others.

Friends: Richard had a feeling of inadequacy about friends (and objectives). Because his moods fluctuated quite a lot, varying from emotional highs to passive lows, he needed the company of those who understood him. It would have been reassuring for him to have had friends on whom he could have depended when occasionally he needed their support.

Family: Richard wanted to show his appreciation for his parent's assistance during his formative years. Perhaps he was simply repaying off a debt that he had incurred from them earlier. There was happiness in domestic conditions but also an uneasy expression of his affections resulting in a lack of harmony. Probably he would have had unusual children but often separated from them. In any case, he showed eccentricity in ways of taking care of anyone (or anything).

Lover: Richard's affections were demonstrative and gay but, being inconstant, he did not want to be enchained. He often preferred freedom to marriage. Unless he was mentally and emotionally composed, he should have avoided early marriage to compensate for his parental insufficiency. Perhaps the environment in which he grew up conditioned him to expect failure in romance, or he may have had strong family ties making it difficult for him to get involved in a personal relationship. Time would have alleviated this problem. However, he didn't function at his best unless he was involved in some kind of relationship. True understanding between himself and his partner was essential if his relationship was to last. There must have been a spiritual bond in addition to the romantic alliance or he would have become increasingly uncomfortable in it. His partner should have realised how important it was for him that he had the opportunity to succeed or fail on his own terms. Partnership, marriage and legacies would have had a major financial impact—sometimes good and sometimes bad. Once involved in a permanent relationship he would have been able to make worthwhile strides in his career and in his other interests. He felt that he must make special efforts to prove himself to the one he loved, as though his personality was not attractive enough, which, of course, was not the case. He would have sought a career that provided a substantial income to satisfy the obligations of a relationship to lessen the pain of being away from the one he loved. The contacts he made through his partner could have given him the opportunity to rise to prominence in his career thus allowing him and his family to have everything that made for a satisfying relationship.

Career

Early: Richard's destiny was in his own hands with a tendency to a lucky journey and good opportunities through life. There was gain through sensational, unusual and adventurous channels as well as from several sources, such as: mining, hidden, the armed forces and uniformed occupations.

It wasn't easy for Richard to gain the career position he wanted because he wasn't sure that he could achieve it on his own. His future success depended on breaking ties with the past, which restrained him, but which was difficult and necessary if he was to become self-sufficient and establish what he owed himself. The most negative thing he could have done was to doubt his ability to do what he wanted with his future, or to believe that he was any less qualified than others. Had he developed a feeling of responsibility for those who were influenced by him, and realised how much they depended on him, he would have become increasingly aware of how much he was needed.

Richard's feeling of insecurity may have developed early in life, when doing what his parents expected meant curtailing his personal desires. This pattern may have made it more difficult for him to establish an independent life for himself. With his creativity he could have secured a place for himself in his career and in society. He needed to have learnt to like himself for his achievements. Few people would have resisted his demands as he strove for an important position. Furthermore, his superiors were impressed with his abilities and he should have had little difficulty getting what he wanted in his career.

Richard had amazing sources of inspiration but he needed training to exploit his creativity for optimum results. In this way he could have capitalised on his innovative creativity by bringing it to the surface ready for use. His talent was free but it would still have taken time and effort to develop it. It wasn't easy for him to make the necessary sacrifices for investing in his career but he knew that it was essential. Even though he knew the importance of education for his career he may not have been willing to make the investment. He expected others to open doors for him but with proper training he could have opened them himself. Although he may have thought twice before spending money for schooling, he did realise that he must stay informed to meet the challenges of his competitors so he continued to educate himself at all times regardless of his formal training.

There was a particular and rather uncompromising direction to his life effort. He had greater ability than there was opportunity to use properly so that success through holding a subordinate position was likely, e.g. a servant, private secretary or agent yet occupying a position of trust. Selling would have been a suitable career and could have shown him how well he performed in dealing with people. He was also suited for occupations dealing with liquids, hospitals, nursing, charity, institutions and prisons. He tended to be a novelist, poet or musician rather than a mathematician or scientist. Alternatively, he could have found a satisfactory career in communications, broadcasting, journalism, social service, public relations, education and perhaps the ministry. Any of these foregoing careers would have brought him into close contact with people who needed his sympathetic understanding. Knowing that he had been helpful could have proved enriching.

<u>Middle:</u> Richard adapted his allegiances to lines along which he could make his efforts count for the most. He was capable of unique achievement through a development of unsuspected relations in life but was also apt to waste his energies through improper alignments with various situations. His willing acceptance of duty brought success through orderly and practical ways even though these may have caused personal limitations and a lack of gaiety. He stayed informed because he knew that made him more valuable in his career. He knew how to capitalise on his training to get attention from people in important positions. In fact he had little difficulty providing the services that his superiors required. They maintained confidence in him, remaining impressed with his growth potential, yet, at times, he must have felt that he was overqualified.

Richard wanted to achieve financial independence so that financial considerations dominated his outlook. He could have succeeded in finance and investment because he understood money, knew how to manipulate his affairs to get the most financial benefits and had a flair for making it serve those who had it. His ability with money won high returns and his intuition became helpful when making investments. His mind calculated the true value of any item before he bought it. He strove to provide services that would have satisfied the most demanding individual and he expected to be well-paid for his efforts. He continued to improve his skills knowing that this would assure him of a steady income. He accepted the daily trials of the real world, knowing that he could have solved any problem that came his way and earned a decent income at the same time.

Richard would have become interested in occupations that brought him before the public. His sensitive understanding of human problems could have been an asset had he decided to earn a living through public service. He had to be cautious, however, and not to allow people to use him as a doormat.

Unfortunately, Richard had a compulsion to achieve through violence in breaking away from existing conditions. The ensuing results often would have caused him further bondage. He may well have suffered great temptation and may have wrecked his life through his conduct. Overall the suggestion is that he led a spiritual life and, despite the tragedy of losing his beloved wife prematurely, the treachery and several other unsuitable conditions alluded to, in the final analysis, a useful one.

Appearance and Health

Appearance: Richard's complexion was soft and pearlescent with mild, meditative, deep and unfathomable eyes. At his worst, his features may have been imperfectly formed with a slack mouth that was loose and ill-finished. In addition, his lower body may not have been well-shaped and so his movement would have seemed clumsy with an indifferent walk and with feet pointing apart like a fish's tail.

Health: Richard had good health in general and was robust physically. His sleep was good with frequent dreams. There may have been a tendency that his energies may have been sapped in ways that would have been difficult to spot. For example, his psychic tendencies could have been unhealthy and difficult to understand. Because he had difficulty breaking past behaviour patterns, he may have become an ulcer-prone individual, who aggravated himself constantly over why the world would not accept him.

- -

Reference: 'Richard II', N. Saul, Yale University Press, New Haven, U.S.A., 1997.

- -

HENRY IV

"I shall strive to rule my people with mercy and truthfulness in all matters."

A first cousin and childhood playmate of King Richard II, both Henry and Richard were admitted together to the Order of the Garter in 1377. However, Henry participated in the Lords Appellant's rebellion against Richard in 1387. After regaining power, Richard did not punish Henry but neither did he forget the role that Henry had played. Henry led two crusading-type expeditions to Vilnius, Lithuania in the early 1390s from where he then undertook a pilgrimage to Jerusalem thereby gaining much worldly experience.

Henry's father, John of Gaunt, died in 1399, whereupon Richard cancelled Henry's inheritance. Henry had been in France and after joining with Thomas Arundel (another former Lord Appellant) they returned to England while Richard was campaigning in Ireland. Henry quickly gained enough power and popular support to have himself declared King Henry IV, imprison Richard (who died there mysteriously) and by-pass Richard's heir presumptive, Edmund de Mortimer. Henry's coronation marked the first time that the new monarch made an address in English.

Henry consulted Parliament frequently but was sometimes at odds with the members on religious matters. Henry spent much of his reign defending himself against plots, rebellions and assassination attempts. For example, there was the Epiphany rising in 1400, the Owen Glyndŵr rebellions in Wales (1400-1415) and, most significantly, the three Percy rebellions from 1402-1408.

The later years of Henry's reign were marked by serious health problems. He developed a disfiguring skin disease but, more seriously, suffered acute attacks of some grave illness from 1405 onwards, until a fatal bout occurred in 1413. Unusually for a King, he was buried at Canterbury Cathedral.

‒ ‒

Speculatively, Henry was born on the 11ᵗʰ April, 1367 NS at 11:09 at Spilsby (Bolingbroke Castle), (see Figure 18) to John of Gaunt and Blanche of Lancaster, both of whom were great, great, grandchildren of Henry III of England and Queen Eleanor of Provence. Thus they were 3ʳᵈ cousins. Again speculatively, Henry's Epoch (see Figure 17) occurred on the 28ᵗʰ July, 1366 NS at 13:45. The planetary distribution of this chart is South indicating objectivity. The overall shaping of the chart is a 'Bucket' with Pluto as an anti-clockwise (conservative) handle and Neptune as a somewhat clockwise (impulsive) one, with the Moon opposite Mars as the bucket's rim. Notice that Pluto in Taurus in the 6ᵗʰ House favourably mediates the bucket's rim. Hence, Henry's utilitarian outlook, his endurance, his obsession with wealth and his enjoyment of the challenge of solving difficult problems are all emphasised. There are two Grand trines in the Epoch chart: one in water having retrograde Venus conjoint Uranus as the focus linked to both Jupiter and Neptune, and one in earth, probably with Pluto as the focus, linked to Mercury and to the Moon. Overall these indicate that Henry was pleasant and at ease with himself but underneath there would have been a struggle for worldly harmony coupled with a sensitiveness to a particular, immediate and practical responsibility. The Sun in Leo—Moon in Capricorn sign polarity shows a hard exterior with much ambition and exactitude that would have been good for business and politics but that inwardly his heart pulled away from externals. The Sun in 9ᵗʰ—Moon in 2ⁿᵈ House polarity re-

Figure 17: Speculative Epoch Chart for King Henry IV.

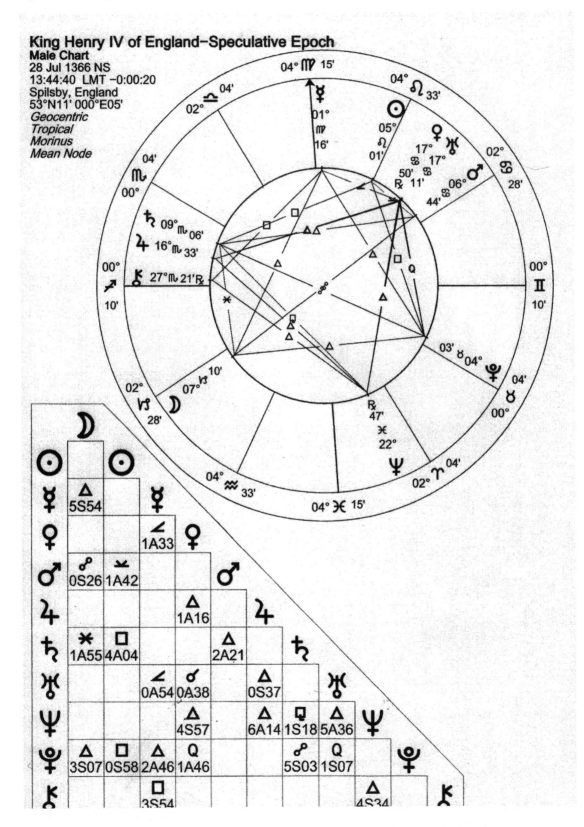

King Henry IV of England–Speculative Epoch
Male Chart
28 Jul 1366 NS
13:44:40 LMT −0:00:20
Spilsby, England
53°N11' 000°E05'
Geocentric
Tropical
Morinus
Mean Node

veals a conflict between asserting himself and apprehension about potential losses. The Sun square Pluto shows a tendency to advance himself ruthlessly and that he wished for self-determination. The Moon opposite to Mars indicates a moody, quarrelsome nature as well as his attraction to successful people, while its trine to Pluto reveals that changes could be made to be favourable and that he wanted people to think well of him. The Morin Point on the border between Scorpio and Sagittarius suggests a hard worker, who could have been both generous and honourable. Jupiter (co-ruler) in Scorpio shows a reserved, yet strong and intense desire for life but a tendency to over-extend himself in grandiose schemes. [We have already mentioned Pluto (co-ruler)]. Retrograde Chiron, rising in Scorpio, indicates that he passionately wanted to give support and help to others secretively, probably because this could have compromised his career interests, but there were favourable results for him from doing this, too.

The Epoch generates his Ideal Birth chart (see Figure 18). Notice that in both charts there are only four quintile family aspects to add support for an intelligence interpretation but other factors would have helped here. For the Birth chart the planets lie mainly to the South indicating objectivity once more. The overall shaping of the chart is 'Splay' that suggests individual, or purposeful, emphases in his life. He acted according to his own special tastes with perhaps an awkward certainty to every approach he made to his life's problems. The Moon, just in Gemini, is bi-semi-square to Uranus and to Venus and suggests much time spent wondering what to do with his life. It also suggests that he was the primary cause of any conflict he faced in his career. Notice that there are two, fairly weak, oppositions in the chart but that these are mediated favourably by the Moon and Mercury separately. The Sun in Aries—Moon in Gemini sign polarity shows manual dexterity and mechanical ability but also restlessness.

Figure 18: Speculative Birth Chart for King Henry IV.

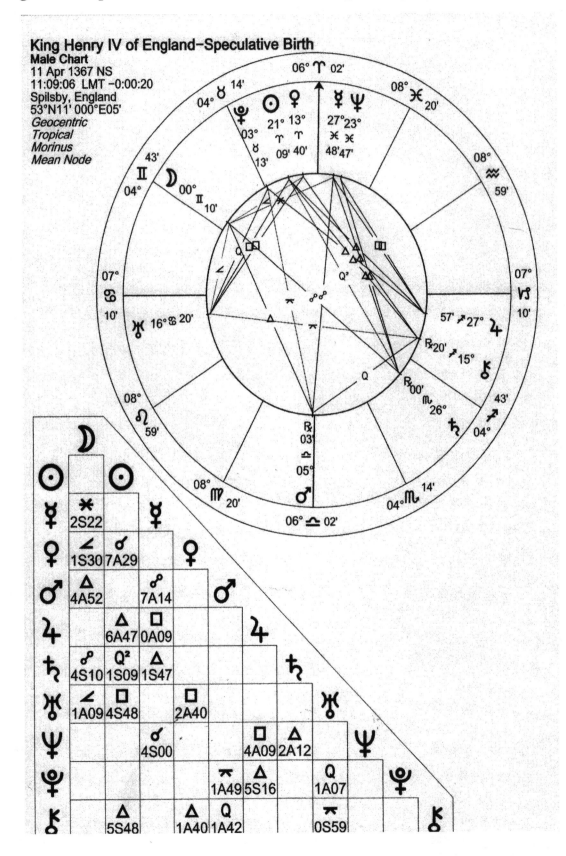

He may have needed periods of inactivity. The Sun in the 11th—Moon in the 12th House polarity shows that he needed to improve his self-image if he was to feel that he deserved reaching his goals. The Sun biquintile Saturn suggests a limitation to his self-expression, probably through his father, and that he needed to make the most of his talent and skills. The Moon sextile Mercury, semi-square Venus and opposition to Saturn shows a good, commonsense mentality and strong intuition, perhaps carried out perversely and with a tendency to overvalue the practical. The Morin Point in the first Cancer decanate shows a love of travel and change as well as a love of home and family that would have been characteristic throughout life. [We have described the Moon (ruler) already]. Uranus in Cancer in the 1st House shows a tendency to be unstable emotionally. He didn't believe in interfering in friend's affairs and he expected the same courtesy from them. Mars retrograde in Libra in the 4th House reveals that not only did he have difficulty identifying his own desires but that he also took on those of others. He tried to relive the emotional experiences of his past and so needed constant encouragement if he was to do something with his future. His inner needs could thoroughly have exhausted those around him.

Character Portrait

General: Henry could well have been generous and honourable, inspiring respect. His feelings were deep and his sympathies wide. As a cheerful and jovial personality, he was a supreme optimist, broad-minded and long on enthusiasm. However, there was a tendency that less was done than was talked about. He had endurance, leadership, a love of power and an ability to organise, govern and rule others. On the practical side, he was active, dextrous manually and mobilised his resources well. Although ambitious, keen and determined, he had a restless personality, which may have been tempered by his easy-going and comfort-loving disposition, that showed a love of travel and change, but also of family and home, that would have been characteristic from youth to old age.

Henry tended to be unstable emotionally due, in part, to his somewhat eccentric personality. He felt limited in his self-expression possibly through his father. As a result, he could become stubborn, defiant, moody, boastful, rash, violent, brooding, unscrupulous, easily provoked and revengeful. His hard, exacting, grasping, selfish, worldly yet careful exterior contained much haughty, overbearing ambition but his heart, inwardly, pulled away from externals. It was also a part of his nature to provide support, help and charity penetratingly, passionately and secretively that could have undermined his career but that also favoured love affairs, investments connected with liquids and imaginative exchanges with his children.

Henry inclined to the artistic and possibly could have developed an interest in metaphysics.

Mentality: Henry was objective with a utilitarian outlook that showed good commonsense, some original talent and a clever mind. However, he did overvalue the practical. He was co-operative, thorough and pensive with an ability to merge ideas. He reserved the right to express himself as he chose, i.e. often in an uncompromisingly dogmatic, presumptuous and quarrelsome manner. His ideals were very high but, if he had been unable to realise his dreams, his actions could well have run in the opposite direction. His ideas and intuitions were strong through heightened receptivity but may have been carried out in a perverse or cantankerous manner. Fortunately, odd and unconventional ideas about life, sex and death were mostly kept secret.

Henry tried to relive the emotional experiences of his past tending to fight his own natural evolution by using a strong, unconscious desire to return to the womb that kept him rooted in an earlier stage that had involved him in a strong, psychological conflict with his father. Every step into the future brought him closer and closer to the womb he had never wanted to leave. Thus, one of his greatest problems was that he tended to foist feelings and reactions onto people based upon past memories of whom they reminded him of. In addition, Henry had an inclination to let matters remain as they were, put up with them and so become patiently conditioned to trying circumstances. Further, he sometimes found it difficult to focus on a subject because his interest wandered.

Lifestyle: All Henry's feelings were based on seeing the world through a "family-like" structure. This provided a shell of protection from within which he could peek out at all he saw around him. Interestingly enough, he also complained that this shell kept him from experiencing all that he could have done. He had a feeling of isolation from the world due to an early residue of lost love. Thus he found it difficult to trust the people he met in his life fully because he saw and sensed in each one the symbolic parts of love that he had been deprived of in the past.

Henry's desire nature powered the need to create future fulfilment now. He felt a great deal of internal intensity, which he didn't release easily. Hence he had a tendency to hide from his own feelings, not wanting to face the wall he put up between his outer and inner life. He had a great deal of impatience as he was not only experiencing the depth of his own needs but was also feeling the influences of other people's needs. This often brought conflict between the manner in which he related to society and the way he truly felt. Not only did he have difficulty identifying his own desires but he took on the desires of others thinking that they were his own. The frustration he met became heightened as he tried to balance harmoniously the different drives and desires coming from all the people he knew. As a result he entered a state of limbo as he felt himself being tossed from one side to the other by the wishes, needs and wants of everyone in his life. Ultimately, this created in him a type of emotional paralysis along with a degree of gullibility towards his external environment. Thus he met difficulty in finding his own centre of being. Basically, he was being forced to know who he was amidst everyone he felt he could be.

Henry may have felt powerfully attracted to men through whom he hoped to find himself. He tried to relate to the assertive/energetic quality of every man he met. Basing too much of his opinion of himself on what elders thought of him, he had to work on developing his own estimation of his self-worth. He expanded himself through ways of reserved, yet strong and intense, desire for life. Everything he did was in a broad perspective, and he was often embarrassed because he couldn't quite live up to his own expectations. He didn't make plans and assumed that everything would turn out for the best. He was also ready to alter his life at too short notice. Thus he tended to overextend himself in grandiose schemes, but he believed in himself and refused to admit defeat. He was overly generous and tended to miss out on many of the benefits he had earned. Hence he tended to go through life doing things the hard way and became envious of others who had reached the same goals with less effort. Overall, he felt a great deal of resentment because he felt cheated, or deprived, of much that he believed was rightfully his.

Henry experienced an intensive struggle for worldly harmony coupled with an overemphasised sensitiveness to a particular, immediate and practical responsibility. There was a specific and uncompromising direction to his life effort containing highly individual, or purposeful, emphases. His obsession was wealth with a compelling need to achieve permanence, although he had no basic desire to conserve himself or his resources. His temperament tended to jut out into experience according to his own special tastes. He had a robust resistance to pigeon-holing either in nature's neat compartments or in his associates' idea pockets. He developed an awkward certainty to every approach he made to life's problems. He dipped deeply into life and poured forth the gathered results of his experiences with unremitting zeal.

Generally, Henry's interests were particular yet impersonal. His ideas on love, art and beauty were 'out-of-the-ordinary', hence more exciting and attractive but there was also a tendency to be "off with the old and on with the new". If spiritual (e.g. literature) rather than physical pleasures were met, then these became both a joy and happiness.

Relationships

<u>Others:</u> Henry was at ease with himself, hence a pleasant person whom others liked to help and favour. Money came from others in unexpected ways. Although an instructor and inspirer of others, he had a tendency to advance himself through ruthless behaviour towards them. Being accepted in the social mainstream was most important to him. He wanted people to consider him responsible and trustworthy. He felt a strong, spiritual responsibility to help others and he derived much inner satisfaction from exploiting his creativity in this way. People looked to him for help with their major problems and his invaluable insight was often sought by important, influential people. However, it went against his grain when anyone suggested that he should adhere to a particular code of behaviour concerning his physical interests. Although it annoyed him to concede to others, whom he knew were wrong, he felt that it was politically advisable and that doing otherwise might jeopardise his chances of being accepted. Once he was established, however, he wouldn't have made such concessions because he considered it unbecoming. He preferred honesty and was perfectly willing to tell people he liked them, if they seemed pleasant and attractive.

Henry was highly perceptive but he didn't like others to see into him. At times, secretly, he would have been jealous of others, who seemed to have more than he did. As he went through life, he seemed to relate better with people whose ages were very different from his own. He gained strength from those older than himself, while, at the same time, tested his own strength on those younger. He could have been an enormous energy drain on others around him as he tended to need their energy to direct himself. His inner needs would have exhausted all those around him.

Friends: Henry had a feeling of inadequacy with friends (and objectives) due partly to frequent breaks with them. He acquired many friends through his career and he used them to gain his objectives. However, he didn't expect friends to yield everything because their desires and future security were as important to them as his were to him. His friends included people who were highly evolved as well as those who were indifferent to development. He didn't interfere in their affairs and he demanded the same courtesy from them. Usually he picked as friends people who were symbolic parent figures. Through these people he would have blamed one of his parents (father?) for all the obstacles that he was unable to surmount in his own life.

Family: Constantly, Henry relived his early childhood relationships with his parents (his mother had died when he was only one). He shouldn't have blamed his father for his problems in getting his career started in what would have been satisfying for him and rewarding for others because his early environment had allowed him to express his creativity. Alternatively, he may have felt that he owed his father so much that he had to put a low priority on his own personal interests. Unless he changed that attitude he would have let precious time pass without focusing on what he owed himself.

Although his relations with his mother may not have been easy, his sense of lack/loss could have generated an "Oedipus Complex", in which he never really understood his love for his mother. He would have kept on asserting that he wanted to be on his own but underneath it all he didn't really know how to let go of the protective feelings he had needed in his childhood.

Henry's affection was sympathetic, tender and somewhat eccentrically maternal and cherishing in his desire to care for loved ones, which was attractive for home-making ways. Thus, home life tended to be harmonious with strong family links, despite being unpeaceful, occasionally. Henry enjoyed his children as they enjoyed him and he knew how to cultivate their desire to live up to their own potential. He demanded the opportunity for his children to develop their potential and the subsequent chance to prove what they could do with it. He even offered himself as an example of what someone could accomplish through individual fulfilment. He himself gave them the chance to exploit their potential to the fullest. He hoped his children would have also learnt generosity and have found enrichment in giving of themselves. Still, his greatest strength would have come in later life when it became important for him to give his own children and grandchildren all the security and comfort around which his own values had been built.

There is an indication that his father would have died young (untrue?) and that he would experience the death of his wife (true).

Lover: Henry had a compelling need to get involved with persons who shared his strong desire for warm, sociable relationships. However, Henry's relations with women were not easy. This sense of lack intensified his shyness and prevented an easy response to what could have brought happiness. He tended to want to share his responsibilities with those he felt were stronger than himself and so he did not truly want to be alone in his life. Henry was usually on his best behaviour, which he considered a good investment to win over someone who attracted him. Although his affections were harmonious, sympathetic, tender but somewhat maternal, he did experiment with feelings. His innovative talents made him a creative lover and his partner probably was quite content with his skill in love making but there may have been difficulty finding someone who felt the same way as he did about not adhering to any particular code of behaviour concerning physical interests. He tried to be understanding of his partner's needs and he was always willing to discuss any problems that came up. If the lines of communication were kept open at all times then he felt that most difficulties could have been resolved.

Henry's sexual drive was related to a strong desire to possess. His emotion of love was often coupled with past anger and resentment directed at some individual experience, which caused painful memories. Sexually he vacillated from periods of intense need to periods of total disinterest.

In marriage Henry projected early feelings towards his parents onto his wife. He may even have married a girl that he thought reminded him of his mother. His mate should have understood that he had to choose his priorities carefully so that he could have devoted enough time and energy to his career while still fulfilling the demands of a marriage. All being well, he should have enjoyed success and happiness in both areas of responsibility.

There is an indication of gain through his partner's, or inherited, money.

Career

Early: Henry's destiny was in his own hands. He was fortunate for money, property, business, politics, and prominent positions. He was one who would have come before the public. Generally, he would have had many opportunities and the expectation of good luck but he was a bit short on applying himself to his goals and there was the possibility for him to meet hardships. However, there was also the tendency for him that changeful happenings, even though violent, could well have been turned to good account.

Henry adapted to job assignments fairly well and learnt new skills easily. He could have achieved the security he wanted only if he had been willing to make the most of his talents and skills. Rather than assume that he could not do something (his creativity should have allowed him to enjoy a fulfilling life) if he had got the right training then that would have qualified him to succeed in it. Once he had gained the credentials he needed, he probably would have become a specialist in some area of endeavour. Freedom was so important to him that nothing would stand in the way of getting the training he needed to achieve future goals and in his view anyone who lacked training was likely to become trapped in a life situation that limited personal privileges or the ability to assert oneself individually. Thus he took every opportunity to improve his skills when special training was available. He eagerly absorbed every bit of information because he knew his career would benefit if he was well informed. He would also have derived greater self-confidence because then he knew he could accept increased responsibility.

Henry himself was the primary cause for any conflicts he faced in achieving his objectives. All the misfortunes and troubles he met could well have been traced to his emotional and hypersensitive nature. He was attracted to successful people and he admired them for gaining freedom from financial worries. However, there was no point in comparing his resources with other people's, unless by doing so it urged him to succeed in his own endeavours. Similarly he had to try not to compare his skills with those of other people because that would have intimidated him.

Henry spent much time pondering what to do with his life. He needed constant encouragement if he was to do something constructive with it. He preferred a career that allowed him self-determination. He wanted to be free to use his creativity in activities that were far removed from the usual, boring routine. He wanted to be self-employed, if possible, but even if he had been employed by others he should have had self-determination in his job. He didn't take to discipline well so his development and growth in his chosen field might have been slow and unpredictable. He wanted the opportunity to develop his potential and prove what he could have done with it. He could have achieved honest success by means of a thrusting, purposeful nature and a capacity for hard work. He had enormous faith that he could have succeeded in anything he attempted and his devotion to his responsibilities made it possible for him to "move mountains". However, reaching the goals he had set depended largely on improving his self-image so that he felt that he had deserved them.

There were many choices available to Henry for selecting a career including law, politics, business administration, education, government service and journalism. He should have selected a career that was sufficiently demanding, which he found stimulating and which fired him with enthusiasm for making the most of his creativity. For example, hospitals, correctional facilities, programs for people who were deaf, dumb and mute, medical, physical therapy and pastoral care all provided areas where understanding and compassion were critical.

Henry also enjoyed the challenge of solving difficult problems. For this reason a career in research and development in such areas as psychology, medicine or industry would have been suitable. He had a talent for improving the techniques used in these areas so that they could serve their objectives better.

Henry's mechanical, travel and literary undertakings were also favoured. Outdoor activities, such as soldiering and naval activities, would have attracted him and given him pleasure.

<u>Middle:</u> Henry was intent on service. He had come to know how to adapt to any circumstances that allowed him to exploit his potential fully. Understandably, he adapted his allegiances to lines along which he could make his efforts count for the most. Thus he was always able to distinguish himself so long as he could prove that his accomplishments were valuable. In this way he could have made a worthwhile contribution and derived a comfortable income. If, in addition, the public had appreciated his efforts he would have felt that he had accomplished something meaningful that was also spiritually satisfying. However, he tended to overextend himself and then stop short when he reflected on the losses he might have suffered by taking unrealistic chances. There developed a constant struggle between his desire to assert himself, confident that success would have followed naturally, and his apprehension about personal or material security. In time, he would have learnt to put this situation into perspective and take action only when the circumstances offered a reasonably high probability of success. By deferring his decision on important matters until he'd had time to examine them thoroughly, he would have avoided a lot of unnecessary grief.

Henry's intellectual awareness of social justice provoked a compassionate response suggesting that he might have worked in an enterprise to offer solutions to social problems. Once he got involved and realised how effective his contribution was, he would have had the foundation on which he could have built a career that was enriching for him and for those he served. He might have met some painful situations, which he could have learnt to handle using his objectivity. However, he tended to hide his talents for working with a wide variety of people in diverse situations to help them to help themselves even though he had the right to expect a reasonable return for his efforts.

Health and Appearance

<u>Appearance:</u> Henry was of middle stature, with a round face, full cheeks, possibly a double chin, dark eyes, medium complexion, and a short nose that may have been prominent at the tip. Later, he would have become rather fleshy and stout with something of a heavy walk.

<u>Health:</u> Henry had an interest in healing possibly because he tended to suffer from indigestion (he had to guard against over-indulging), poor health and poor recuperation. His deep concern about the future may have affected his health if he had not allowed time for indulgence in personal pleasures. Some rest may have been needed to restore harmony to his system. Nervous (cantankerous), mental or inner struggles were possible but he did have thought control. In addition, he may have been prone to deep-seated or infectious diseases. Furthermore, there may have been a liability to rheumatism, heart or stomach problems. Although an easy death was indicated (possibly through blood diseases, e.g. diabetes), there was also an indication for a quick, sudden and painful death through fever, accident or nervous trouble.

- -

Reference: 'The Fears of Henry IV—The Life of England's Self-Made King', Ian Mortimer, J. Cape, London, 2007.

- -

HENRY V

"Some sons of iniquity . . . wickedly suggested . . . that I would seize my father's royal regalia . . . to which he had no proper title."

At the time of Henry's birth, the king was his father's cousin, Richard II. After military experience fighting various lords who rebelled against his father, King Henry IV, Henry came into political conflict with his increasingly ill father and king. When his father died in 1413, Henry rapidly assumed control of the country and embarked on war with France. After an unassuming start, his military successes in the Hundred Years' War, culminating with his famous victory at the Battle of Agincourt, saw him come close to conquering France. Following months of negotiations with King Charles VI of France, the Treaty of Troyes recognised Henry V as regent and heir-apparent to the French throne. Subsequently, he married Charles' daughter, Catherine de Valois. After Henry V's sudden death in France (of dysentery?), he was succeeded by his infant son, who reigned as King Henry VI.

Henry was the eldest son (of four) of King Henry IV of England (born before his father became king) and Mary de Bohun. He was born on the 24th September, 1386 NS at 11:27 at Monmouth, Wales (see Figure 20). His Epoch occurred on the 11th December, 1385 NS at 07:05 (see Figure 19). The Epoch chart shows that the planets lie mainly to the South (above the Earth) and East indicating objectivity and that his destiny lay mainly in his own hands. The overall planetary shaping is 'Splay' suggesting highly individual, or purpos-

Figure 19: King Henry V's Epoch Chart

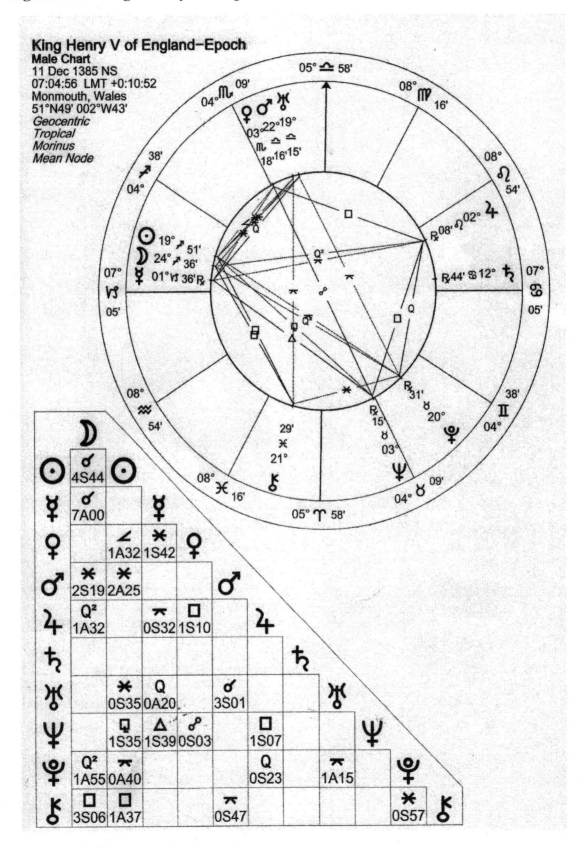

eful, emphases in his life coupled with his own special tastes.

There is a fixed T-square with Jupiter at the focus, i.e. bi-square Venus and Neptune, showing that he tended to let difficulties remain as they were and put up with them. Additionally, there are two contiguous Yods, one with Pluto at the focus bi-quincunx to the Sun and the Uranus/Mars conjunction, and the second with the Uranus/Mars conjunction bi-quincunx to Pluto and Chiron. The transformative nature of a Yod indicates that Henry either felt compelled to take advantage of opportunities presented to him, or had to take himself firmly in hand to avoid personal disasters. Moreover, there was a quintile family Yod with the Moon as the focus bi-biquintile to Jupiter and Pluto. This indicates that he willingly helped people who needed his tender, loving care. The Sun and Moon both in Sagittarius sign polarity shows too much independence and too great a love of freedom yet also an inclination towards conservatism. The Sun in the 12th—Moon in the 1st House polarity reveals that his life efforts should really have been focused on improving the quality of life for those people unable to help themselves.

The Sun sextile Uranus reinforces his independence making him more interesting, dramatic, scientific, magnetic and perhaps rebellious. The Sun square Chiron indicates difficulty providing help to others and that, if he had got to the top, it would have been as a result of careful planning and meticulous work. The Moon sextile Mars shows excellent strength both physically and emotionally with an ability to work hard, push on in life and his need for friends, who could have shared his emotional highs and lows. The Morin Point in the 1st Capricorn decanate shows a self-controlled personality capable of achieving success through hard work, practical abilty, a shrewd mind and inner stability. Notice particularly that the ruler (Saturn) is setting, retrograde, in its detriment, Cancer, in the 7th House and, seemingly, unaspected. This presents a difficult problem for interpretation. The unaspected case would indicate either: all control, or none, and/or a lack of moral sense. Further interpretations of Saturn's situation may not be valid because its principle is not well-integrated with the rest of Henry's personality. However, closer examination reveals a septile within 1^0 of exactness between Saturn and Pluto. A septile suggests an ability to change levels. Thus, the deepened concentration interpretation of a Saturn-Pluto aspect here means that Henry could deepen his level of concentration when the situation required it and this fits in well with the 'deep thinker' interpretation of retrograde Mercury rising in Capricorn (see following). Now that Saturn has an aspect that integrates its principle, at least in part, with the rest of his personality then we can suggest that interpretations such as: 'misfortunes and many obstacles will beset his path', 'he needed security and kept dwelling on emotions that burdened his past' and 'he felt that a spouse would hold him back' would now apply.

Notice also that retrograde Mercury is rising in Capricorn. This shows that he was a deep and weighty thinker who tried too hard to pinpoint his exact meaning. His thought was focused on child-like expectations of self-progress and so tended to come into association with those who were young and immature.

The Epoch chart generates his Ideal Birth chart (see Figure 20). There are seven quintile family aspects present in both charts to support the interpretation of good intelligence. For the Birth chart the planetary distribution is to the South and to the West indicating objectivity and that his destiny was mainly in the hands of others/ circumstances. The overall planetary shaping is a 'Bucket' in which Mars in Capricorn in the 2nd House is the anticlockwise handle planet to the Mercury/Sun conjunction—Chiron opposition that forms the Bucket's rim. This means that there was a particular and uncompromising direction to his life-effort, in which energy and initiatory force were spent conservatively with a keen desire to plan

Figure 20: King Henry V's Birth Chart.

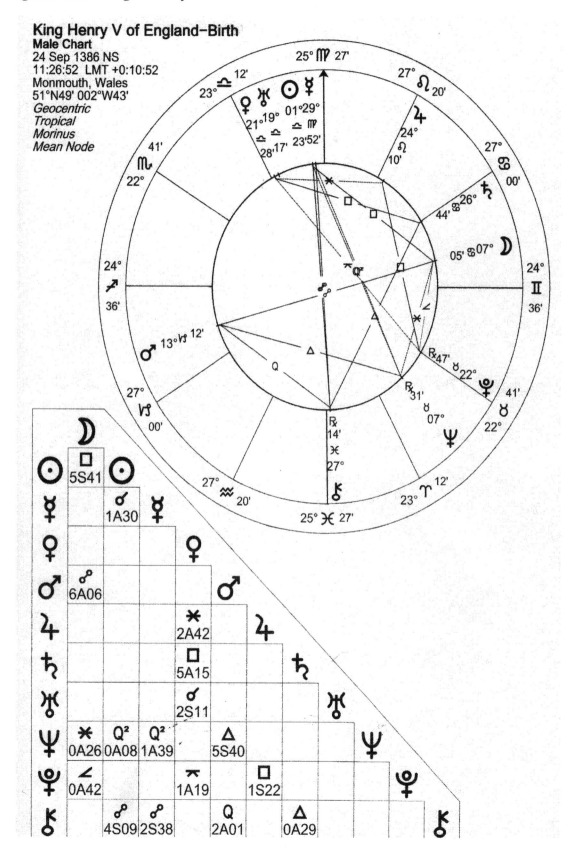

King Henry V of England–Birth
Male Chart
24 Sep 1386 NS
11:26:52 LMT +0:10:52
Monmouth, Wales
51°N49' 002°W43'
Geocentric
Tropical
Morinus
Mean Node

and succeed in acquisitive, financial and possibly agricultural ways. The Sun in Libra—Moon in Cancer sign polarity shows that he was anxious, especially regarding home affairs, but also initiatory. The Sun in 10th—Moon in 7th House polarity shows that success in his career brought him personal satisfaction, status before the public and would have improved his self-image. The Sun conjoint Mercury reveals that he was responsive to public opinion and also that he felt a strong obligation to help others. The Sun biquintile Neptune shows his affinity for all affairs connected with the sea and the Moon sextile Neptune implies that his imagination gave out much through the reception of ideas and influences. The Morin Point in the 3rd Sagittarius decanate indicates a generous, honourable character that inspired respect with a strong dominating interest in women. Jupiter (the ruler) sextile Venus shows popularity through sheer, innate charm and so many happy love affairs. On the other hand, Jupiter square Pluto indicates a compulsive desire to break away from existing conditions that tended, unfortunately, to cause further bondage.

Character Portrait

General: "Duality" is a keyword for describing Henry's character. His outer nature was quite different from his inner one. As a generous, honourable character that inspired respect, his only real drawback was a tendency to be self-righteous and priggish. His self-expression was noble, dignified, loyal, high-minded and good-hearted but occasionally exaggeratedly bumptious. In addition, he expected too much independence with too great a love of freedom that included tendencies to become reckless, rebellious and, just possibly, moody or quarrelsome. At the same time there were inclinations to be conservative but a love of travel, science, philosophy and religion was strongly marked. Any paradoxical results of disruptiveness were expressed through harmonious ways. He was charming and lovable though somewhat odd in expressing this. Thus his temperament jutted out into experience according to his own special tastes. He showed a robust resistance to pigeon-holing either in nature's neat compartments or in associates' idea pockets.

On the other hand, Henry showed an ability to work and push on in life. As a persistent, self-reliant, self-controlled and strong personality emotionally, he was capable of achieving success through his practical ability combined with a shrewd mind. Yet, there was an inclination to let matters remain as they were and to put up with them, so that he became patiently conditioned to trying circumstances. Being acquisitive, he may have amassed considerable possessions. On the other hand, he may have lacked humour, humility, spontaneity, consideration and warmth.

Henry was attracted to music, art, dancing, acting, psychism, the spiritual, the mystical and to hidden things. He was interested in all matters to do with the sea. These he pursued with energy and work was done to satisfy his desire to experiment in new ways.

Mentality: Henry's thought was focused on the expectation of self-progress. He had a child-like quality in that many received energies were redirected inwards to a focus on himself. Not understanding how to refocus his mental energies outward, he became a part of all he projected. Thus, he had difficulty knowing where he ended and the outer world began. His biggest problem was finding out who he really was, for he was constantly sifting through, and questioning, his own identity. Again, like a child, he was highly impatient to find out. Never waiting for the understanding of the world to come to him, he rushed into it, to know all he could—yesterday. He stampeded into situations, jumping to conclusions, which needed correction later, only to retreat into himself once he was there. Even then, he had difficulty measuring what he knew when he had found out what he thought he was looking for. Overall, there was clearly a continuous, fluctuating element of mental uncertainty here.

Henry's mind and relatively narrow mental outlook was improved as far as charm of speech, pleasantness of manner and the benefit of an harmoniously working nervous system were concerned. However, balance rather than worry, and ease rather than strength, were gained. This favoured his diplomatic ability and his subtlety of mind. Impressions came to his mind so that it became the channel for all inspirations, ideas and dreams. There was a changeableness coupled with a desire for progress here but his psychic, prophetic and predictive qualities may have been overshadowed by his ambitious tendencies. Additionally, he was objective, interesting and possibly rebellious with inclinations to success in inventive, flashing, scientific thought, in leadership and in any of the more profound areas of study. He had capacities for deep concentration, deliberation, tenacity, persistence and even defiance. His speech was quick and dramatic. Occasionally, woolly thinking, indiscretion and poor judgement as a result of a lack of concentration (see Health) that could have made it difficult for him to focus on an objective. These qualities could have caused him to become irritable, suspicious discontented and penetrative. In addition, the duality of his nature probably showed out strongly causing occasional indecision of mind as well as changes of direction in his mode of life.

On the other hand, Henry was a very deep and weighty thinker. Having once made a mistake, he had the ability to understand it on a deep level with a great sense of perspective. He could then have approached the source, or a similar construct, again and made it work correctly. His greatest strength occurred when, seeing his crystallised thought from his past, he was able to absorb more knowledge for future building. In all things he always considered the end result before he could have even contemplated the steps he might have taken towards achieving it. Thus, he was highly pragmatic and practical.

He did not lead a spontaneous life because it was easier for him to be more in tune with the purpose of his own thought patterns than with the natural flow of forces in the world around him. Self-expression was difficult for him because he tried too hard to pinpoint his exact meaning. Thus, he only liked to talk about things that were meaningful, serious, or which represented sobriety. Accordingly, one of his greatest difficulties lay in personal communications as others tended to lose patience with all he was trying to build. In the first half of his life, he could have gone through paranoid periods in which he got bogged down in his own depth. Still, he was more than able to plod his own way back out. Later in life, he was more easily understood after the weight of his thinking had found suitable outlets in traditional society.

Lifestyle: Living for the moment, as Henry did, it was imperative to concentrate more on his goals and objectives. His creativity could have failed him unless he realised how important it was to develop his talents. He hated the confinement of a daily routine because it inhibited his freedom but he wouldn't have become really free until he applied himself and earned it. Being independent, there were highly individual, or purposeful, emphases in his life. There was an awkward certainty to every approach he made to his life's problems. He dipped deeply into life and poured forth the gathered results of his experiences with unremitting zeal. He was interested in a cause but not so concerned over end-results, himself or his resources. However, he did know the steps that had to be taken to achieve anything substantial and would have drawn on his early, past-life knowledge again and again in order to try to convey this to others, who were always looking for the easy way out.

There were particular yet impersonal interests in his life in which pleasurable activities often exerted an attraction, especially those involving travel or an outdoor life.

Relationships

<u>Others:</u> Henry was generally popular due to his ease of attracting others, the public and superiors by sheer, innate charm that would have led to success. He was most responsive to public opinion and became distressed if it ever became unfavourable. When he liked people, he didn't hesitate to tell them so, and they responded eagerly to his honesty. But, at other times, in his desire for communication, he was less objective so that his flattery was misdirected. Simply put, he wanted people to like him. However, he was apprehensive about being accepted by others because he didn't think that he could live up to their expectations and so he tended to come into association with those who were young and immature. If he had developed his creativity, then could have easily fitted into any social environment because he'd established his worth to society. Some of the tension he felt with other people came from his early conditioning about loyalty to his parents rather than to anyone outside his family. Sometimes he made concessions to people that were painful to his ego and he felt that the best way to avoid this problem was to gain respect and admiration for his professional achievements. As a career orientated person he would have met many people from various walks of life through his professional affairs. Therefore he must have learnt how to cope with them, so that his professional development would have been enhanced by the support they could have given him. He became a real instructor and inspirer of others. However, his support, help and charity was provided intangibly, and with difficulty, to others. Similarly, his response to support, help and charity provided by others was also difficult. On the other hand, he willingly helped people who needed his tender, loving care. In fact, he was too eager to be available when someone said they needed him, perhaps because he wanted human companionship at any cost. Actually, he should have directed some of his energy to developing his own creativity and sacrificed

some of his time that he spent on others, if he had wanted to, because, overall, he had to remember to put himself at the top of the list of his priorities.

<u>Friends:</u> Henry's many friends were very important to him. He needed friends who could share his emotional highs and lows. Unfortunately, he tended to be suspicious of friends, assuming they wanted his friendship only because he was willing to do favours for them.

<u>Family:</u> Henry had an anxious, sympathetic and domesticated disposition especially regarding home affairs. His parental nature, his attraction to family and to his relations, was strong. His desire for security, and the realisation of a need for caution, resulted in a strong feeling for guarding and cherishing those who were under his care. He provided support, help and charity energetically, thoughtfully and efficiently to home affairs, family and parents. There was only a slight tendency to be unpeaceful at home. Although it would have been difficult, he would have managed to satisfy his responsibilities to his children and still have had a career that would have satisfied his desire to achieve recognition for his services. He also hoped to encourage his children to take advantage of the opportunities he provided so that they too would reach their goals. His children would have been aware of his success and would have followed his example to assert themselves according to their own needs. Regrettably, his children may have been unfortunate.

<u>Lover:</u> Henry had a strong interest in women, an interest that was mingled with a desire for domination and his popularity with them would have led to success. He was demonstrative and ardent in affection, falling in love often and expressing his sympathetic, sensitive and kind-hearted nature. His love affairs were numerous and very happy and his partnerships beneficial and very successful.

However, he may have grown up feeling hesitant about extending himself to people whom he was attracted to, unless he was sure that his parents would have approved. To avoid this problem he focused his attention on career interests. This situation would have improved as and when he met more people with similar interests. But there was frustration and disappointment to be expected from others in close connection whether in marriage or business. This strengthened him by building his ability to stand on his own two feet (or, more unlikely, depressed him from loneliness because of inadequacy in forming happy relationships). He may have married early to challenge the conditions at home, but the chance of a marriage succeeding on that basis was doubtful. It would have been better to wait until he was established and secure in his profession or business.

Career

Early: As a deeply responsive person, Henry was profoundly influenced by both positive and negative forces in his immediate environment. This vulnerability may have resulted from his early conditioning when he could have done little without parental approval, although, at times, he may have been criticised for not taking the initiative. A feeling of uncertainty and apprehension may have developed from this that made it difficult for him to feel comfortable in asserting himself. His parents probably made some sacrifices so that he could have pursued his own course in life more easily. The legacy of influence from his parents was a firm base from which to achieve independence and security by his own efforts. He appreciated the advice and effort he had received in his early years and so he didn't mind making sacrifices for them later, although he did realise how important it was to build a foundation for his own accomplishments first.

Henry's destiny was in his own hands but also in the hands of others as well as depending on prevailing conditions. His fate was affected by his moral growth, his power to organise and by his ability to rise above the difficulties of his early environment. Early on he seemed to do things the hard way but this helped him to achieve later. At first, there may have been painful moments when he competed with qualified people, who tried to intimidate him. He mustn't have underestimated what he could have done and have remembered that any reversal or failings along the way would have taught him more than he could have learnt in any other way. Probably, he was impatient to grow up because he was anxious to prove he could succeed if given the opportunity. He had thought a great deal about finding the right focus for his energies to obtain maximum results from his creativity. It became urgent that he examined his creativity and determined which parts could have been developed into the skills that he needed to be effective in his career. Thus, he had developed many ideas for gaining a good position with all its benefits. Realising that his rise to prominence would have required a great deal of creative effort, he tried to utilise all his talents to achieve it. He then offered it to important people when seeking their attention. He knew how to improve on traditional methods and the results he got enhanced his position. Some position of trust, or responsibility, advanced his interests and depending on the self-possession, tact and prudence he displayed, he made successful progress thereby gaining recognition, fame and honour. If he had got to the top of his field, then it would have been through careful planning and meticulous work.

Henry disliked working at ordinary jobs that didn't make sufficient demands on his talent. It wasn't that he was afraid of hard work because he knew that would make him that much more valuable to his superiors and to himself. It was rather that he didn't really believe in his ability to get what he wanted out of life. Yet he didn't give in to problems. He had vigorous ambition and worked towards an end with a keen desire to plan and succeed. Thus, there was a particular and uncompromising direction to his life effort in which he adapted his allegiances to lines along which he could make his efforts count for the most. He became a leader in the affairs of the world with vision and readiness to change old ways.

Middle: Henry planned secretly how to promote his ideas for the greatest gain as he was always looking for better ways to use his creativity. There were opportunities that, seemingly, he felt compelled to take advantage of. Thus, he was able to capitalise on his latent talents especially when there was gain through favours and through powerful friends. On the other hand, he might have needed to take himself thoroughly in hand to avoid falling deeply into trouble. Misfortune and many obstacles may have beset his path, for example sorrow through superiors, forlorn hopes and peculiar experiences. In addition, he had a compulsive desire to achieve through violence in bursting away from existing conditions, the results of which often caused him further bondage.

He had to learn to work to serve the needs of others. His life effort should really have been focused on the quality of life for people who were unable to help themselves. His love of people and his high ideals would have enabled him to develop a strong obligation and responsibility to share his skills with those who wanted to improve their station in life. His healing ability could have helped to lessen the unacceptable conditions that diminished man's dignity. He would have been an asset to society if he had accepted his duties and not have minded working behind the scenes where the problems arose. The satisfaction of making worthwhile contributions would have improved his self-image, given him status before the public and enriched him with the feeling of having fulfilled a useful role. He would have continued to develop as long as his objectives were related to those of society.

<u>Vocation:</u> He should have seriously considered a career that would have brought him into contact with people especially if they depended on the services he offered. The limited visibility of such a calling may not have appealed to him but his accomplishments would have more than compensated for this by allowing him the privilege of greater privacy in his affairs. He could have become a writer, visionary artist, poet, dancer, mimic, mystic, medium or spiritualist. Some careers that would have been appropriate for him include business management, public relations, sales, government service, law, politics, family planning and counselling.

Henry expended effort and energy on financial affairs (and also for agriculture?). He may have found it exciting to have an opportunity to handle other people's assets. Financial counselling might have provided an attractive career for him.

<u>Late:</u> He should have started to think about becoming independent so that he could sustain himself in his later years and reach the goals that he had chosen. He dwelt on the future and worried about whether he would be financially secure in his later years. By servicing the needs of others he would have gained the financial security he needed for later on.

Health and Appearance

<u>Appearance:</u> Henry was tall, slender, well-formed with a thin, long nose, hazel eyes, powerful voice, fresh complexion and brown hair with a tendency to baldness near the temples. In profile, he was hatchet-faced but he may have become more favoured after middle age.

<u>Health:</u> Henry's occasional poor judgement probably was due to a lack of correct working between his liver and his nervous system. Although he had excellent strength physically, he should have

understood when to conserve his energy in order to avoid exhaustion. Restraint was needed so that he didn't exceed his physical limits (by too much hard work for others?). There were possibilities for unusual, infectious and deep-seated diseases. Death may have occurred in old-age from a long-standing complaint, or from natural causes (e.g. over-indulgence, liver complaint or carelessness).

- -

Reference: "The Life and Times of Henry V", P. Earle, G. Weidenfeld and Nicholson Ltd., London, U.K., 1972.

- -

HENRY VI

"Burgundy is the one man in the world on whom I would wish to wage war because he abandoned me in my boyhood, despite all his oaths to me, when I had never done him any wrong." (1456)

Henry was King of England (at nine months) from 1422 to 1461 and again from 1470 to 1471. Up until 1437 his realm was governed by regents as he was a child king. He was also the disputed King of France from 1422 to 1453. Accounts of the time described him as peaceful and pious, and so not suited for the dynastic 'Wars of the Roses', which began during his reign. His periods of insanity and his inherent benevolence eventually required that his wife, Margaret of Anjou, had to assume control of his kingdom, which contributed to his downfall, the collapse of the House of Lancaster, and the subsequent rise of the House of York. Henry's one lasting achievement was his fostering of education; he founded Eton College and King's College, Cambridge. According to tradition, he was murdered as he knelt at prayer in the Tower of London, where he had been imprisoned.

- -

Henry was the only child, son and heir of King Henry V of England and Queen Catherine of Valois, France. He was born on the 15th December, 1421 NS, at 16:04 at Windsor, England (see Figure 22). His Epoch (see Figure 21) occurred on the 17th March, 1421 NS, at 10:02. For the Epoch chart, the planetary distribution is East, South and North indicating that his destiny lay in his own hands and that he was both objective and subjective. The overall chart shaping is a

Figure 21: Epoch Chart for King Henry VI of England.

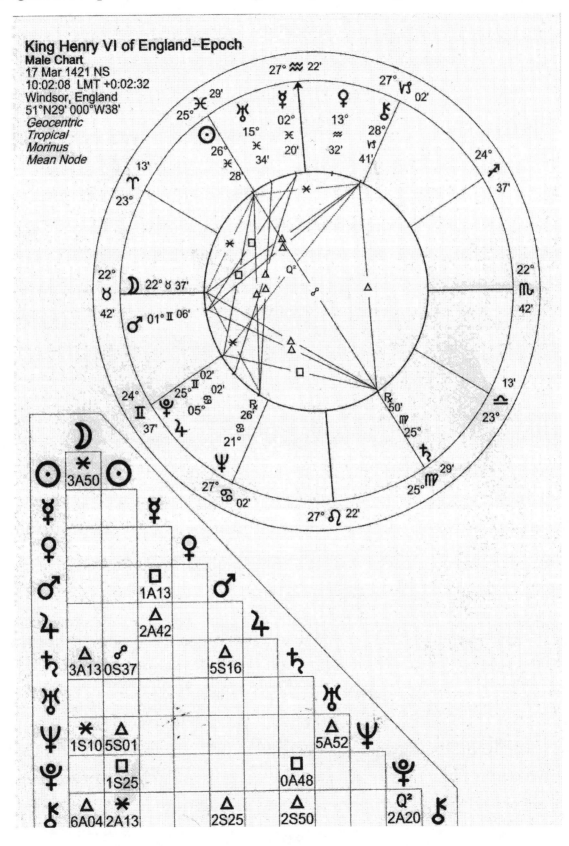

'Bucket' with Saturn as the somewhat clockwise handle planet with Neptune and Chiron as the unconnected rim. This suggests that he tried, somewhat impulsively, to reach past ideals but simultaneously felt a strong need to overcome obstacles first. There would have been a particular and rather uncompromising direction to his life-effort. Specific Interplanetary Aspect Patterns included a Grand-Trine-in-Earth Kite with Saturn at the focus showing an immediate and practical responsibility with a tendency to conform always for the convenience of others. There was also a mutable T-Square with Pluto as the focus of the kite's Sun-Saturn opposition suggesting an adjustment to difficulties, and an attempt to by-pass them, but rarely without nervous stress. The Sun in Pisces—Moon in Taurus sign polarity shows sensitivity and a kind, quiet, pleasant nature with some love of money. The Sun in the 11th—Moon in 1st House polarity suggests fluctuating moods and a need for understanding friends. In addition, he should have avoided marrying too early. The Sun opposition Saturn shows limited self-expression but pride in not having to resort to questionable practices along with a pre-occupation of giving his children every opportunity. The Sun square Pluto indicates a ruthless approach to others, within which he was determined to make the most of what he had in a struggle for financial independence. The Sun sextile the Moon shows an harmonious nature and its sextile to Chiron in the 9th House shows support given to education. The Moon sextile Neptune (and to the Sun) indicates good receptivity and imagination with an interest in the arts and in the affairs of the sea. The Moon bi-trine Saturn and Chiron shows a willing acceptance of duty and that support to education was reciprocated favourably. The Morin Point in the 3rd Taurus decanate reveals friendliness, cheerfulness and a love of pleasure with some ambition and an inclination to run in a groove. Interestingly, Venus (ruler) in Aquarius in the 10th House, is largely unaspected (there is a tredecile to Mars indicating a strengthened love-life and two undeciles to Uranus and Pluto indicating gentility).

This suggests that friendship was preferred to emotional ties and that love was unemotional and detached. He had a desire for humanitarian harmony for others. Mars in Gemini in the 1st House and square to Mercury suggests that his energy was frittered away in constant direction changes and that his mind could be stressed to the point of breakdown. Mars bi-trine weakly to Saturn and to Chiron shows a strong desire to make an impression on the world. We have already mentioned the interpretation of the Moon rising in Taurus.

The Epoch chart generates the Ideal Birth chart (see Figure 22). Notice that there are only three quintile family aspects altogether in both charts to support an interpretation of good intelligence. Notice also that the Epoch and Birth charts both have the Morin Point rising in the 3rd Taurus decanate. This situation is reminiscent of the charts for Edward III and for Richard II. Once again, interpretation here is simplified but also reinforced. For the Birth chart the planetary distribution is general, i.e. the interpretation would be that Henry was both objective and subjective and that his destiny lay in his own hands, in the hands of others as well as depending on prevailing circumstances. The overall shaping of the chart could be 'Splash' indicating 'scatter' but there is also a 'See-Saw' element (three oppositions) from the North East to the South West quadrant showing indecision and a tendency to act at all times under a consideration of opposing views. However, he would have been capable of unique achievement through a development of unexpected happenings in life. Special Interplanetary Aspect Patterns include a distorted kite formation around the Venus (ruler) to Jupiter quincunx that completes a Yod by the sextile to Uranus, which is mediated favourably by the semisextile to Mercury that, in turn, is trine to Jupiter. This suggests a zest for life accompanied by the pride of trying to live a moralistic life. It also suggests a time in childhood when he was able to shine. Separately, there is also a Yod with Pluto

Figure 22: Birth Chart for King Henry VI of England.

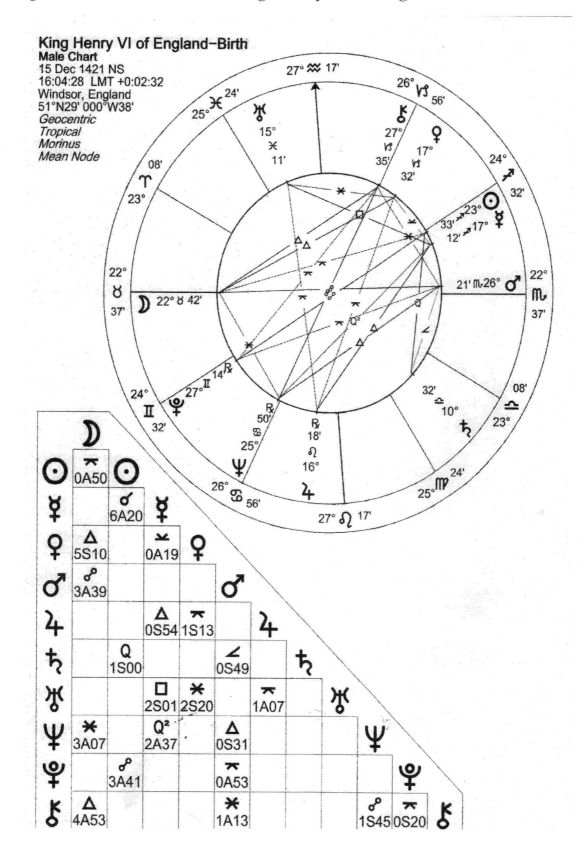

at the focus that is bi-quincunx to Chiron and to Mars suggesting that he had to use fortitude to resist getting what he wanted through collusion or through issuing ultimatums. Notice that there is almost a third Yod with the broad Sun—Mercury conjunction as the focus that is bi-quincunx to the Moon and to Neptune. This could suggest his deep concern for people and a commitment to satisfy their needs. The Sun in Sagittarius—Moon in Taurus sign polarity suggests sympathy coupled with reliable foresight whereas the Sun in 8th—Moon in 1st House polarity shows that an important part of his life was getting involved with the circumstances of others' needs. Of the three oppositions in the chart, only the Sun opposition Pluto fails to receive any favourable mediation. This confirms the interpretation of his ruthless behaviour towards others. In fact, overall, the Sun in the 8th House is poorly aspected, which could suggest the premature death of his father. The Moon opposition to Mars indicates a moody or quarrelsome nature but is mediated favourably by both Neptune and Chiron; it always seemed that he had to make concessions to others. We have already covered the Morin Point lying in the 3rd Taurus decanate with the Moon rising there. Venus (the ruler) in Capricorn in the 9th House shows that Henry was sincere, stable and conventional in affection yet somehow intriguing and fascinating (Venus sextile Uranus). He would have been fond of study.

Character Portrait

<u>General:</u> Basically, Henry could have been very happy in his life in this world. He had a kind, quiet and pleasant nature with some love of money yet very hospitable, genteel, sociable, genial and agreeable. His personality was friendly and cheerful. There was a love of pleasure and social life that helped to bring popularity but a tendency to be too easy-going could have led to difficulties unless it was kept firmly under control. There was some ambition, a fondness for fame and

for public recognition. There was also a desire for change, a love of novelty and much curiosity. However, strong personal feelings coupled with brooding over imagined wrongs and insults could have made him moody or quarrelsome. Although he wasn't a talkative person, he did enjoy discussing important matters. He was fond of study, intelligent interests and travel. He sought knowledge avidly knowing that in his career doors were likely to be open if he was well-informed.

On the other hand, Henry's self-expression was limited, causing self-pity. He tended towards steadiness, conscientiousness and some seriousness. Life seemed rigorous, or hard, so that he became obstinate and fixed with an inclination to run in a groove, or become too conventional, thus making for a laborious and over-cautious approach to problems. Control, patience, balance, reason and necessity came to be expected as experience. Yet his nature tended to be at one with itself, contained some intellectual quality plus stimulated reason thereby mitigating his otherwise intuitive nature. He showed willing acceptance of duty, learnt self-control and gained success through orderly and practical ways even though these may have caused personal limitations and a lack of gaiety. There was a patient working out of what was begun but not with ease. His results had to be battled for. Accordingly, narrowness was engendered and sternness developed.

Henry was self-centred; he felt he knew his abilities as well as his limits, simply because he felt inadequate. He behaved with propriety guided by a fairly strong code of ethics. He didn't indulge himself very much because he was so concerned with self-preservation. He felt that he had to make more sacrifices than others did to get the same results. For this reason he withdrew and concentrated on his own interests, ignoring the rest of the world. He didn't want anyone to be suspicious of his motives, nor did he feel that he needed to explain his actions to others. He also hated to reveal his creativity for similar reasons. He should have bent a little and enjoyed life more. He had a lot to offer the world but restrained himself by worrying about money.

Sensitive, Henry may have given out much through the reception of ideas and influences. As he was highly imaginative, art, psychism, the occult and a love of the sea were all favoured. However, although he had the ability to love all things of beauty, his artistic inclinations did not blend well with reason, action or control.

Mentality: Henry had a cheerful, humorous and witty mentality that brought success through its exercise. His mind and mental outlook were enhanced in so far as charm of speech and pleasantness of manner were concerned. Balance rather than worry was evident and ease rather than strength was gained. His mind was earnest, sympathetic, peaceful, vital and clear to receive well. Being both objective and subjective, his intuitional mind tended to be confused by practical issues but was highly receptive to artistic, psychic and benevolent ideas. His obsession was mobility. More negatively, he could be inscrutable, unscrupulous, incomprehensible, sarcastic, critical and bluffing. Under stress, his mind and nervous system, despite ease, could have become energised to the point of overstrain causing irritability, temper, incisiveness that became satirical and carping, and ultimately breakdown.

It was difficult for Henry to become detached from his thoughts because most of his awareness was of a purely personal nature. He could have become so intent about discovering the truth of all he did not yet understand that he kept looking at himself too closely so that he could no longer see the wood for the trees. He would have understood himself better when he realised why his need to hold himself down was stronger than his need to experience the outer world.

Henry had a gift for seeing to the bottom of problems and dug deep into analysis. He was overly concerned with details that shaped his life, through which he created the order that made sense to him. He kept trying to reach back to past ideals and so inadvertently pre-programmed his perception of things so that they could fit into his ready-made concepts. He tried to fit all the separate parts of the world into all that he formed within himself from his past. Thus he was forced to live in the idealised world he would have liked to see around himself. This made him unusually rigid. However, once he had become sensitive to how unrealistic some of his expectations were, he would have become more comfortable with the world as it actually was. The perfection that already exited there, then would have become apparent to him.

Henry believed that he could teach everybody how to live. He thought of himself as noble, based on having stood earlier for some idea or principle. He liked to think that everything he did in life stood for progress and so he kept spreading himself out to increase the quantity of all he thought was worthwhile. He was attracted to all in life that gave the appearance of reward. One of his weaknesses consisted of the haste with which he jumped to conclusions so that he had to re-evaluate his judgement later. He could have been more out-of-touch with his true nature than he knew. However, as his inflated ego began to diminish he would have become able to experience a very beautiful view of the world.

Unfortunately, he had to come to realise that most of what he was holding onto, and seeking, had little basis in the reality of what truly would have made him happy in his life. He was living through a mental bondage, either by being chained to society's values and/or to his earlier life's obsessive thoughts, which he had to bring to the surface in order to eliminate them. In this way, he would have had to destroy his previous value systems if he was ever going to reach that future happiness. Initially, he had not seen the world clearly and so blamed external factors for depriving him of all that he wanted. (Although, in fact, he may rarely have got what he wanted, in reality he always had what he needed!) As a result, he became highly possessive, unbelievably stubborn and amazingly resistant to any external encouragement, which tried to get him to fit in with the world around him. He preferred to see the world fit his ideals and so lived in his self-created bonds, silently scorning all those who disagreed with his ideas.

Lifestyle: Henry applied a dynamic drive to the process of regeneration that he identified as central to his understanding and to all his personal struggles. Energy was spent on personal affairs quickly and with strong action but his force was frittered away in constant changes of direction because he was restless. He was interested in a cause but he was not that concerned about end-results and had little desire to conserve either himself or his resources. He made adjustments to difficulties, and attempted to by-pass them, but rarely without nervous stress. He had a tendency to act at all times under a consideration of opposing views that had its existence in a world of conflicts. He dipped deeply into life and poured forth the results of his gathered experiences with unremitting zeal.

Henry had a deep respect for the value of money, but he also understood that he had to maintain sound ethical standards in dealing with the public otherwise his material gains would have seemed tainted. Probably he'd worked hard to learn as much as he had and he prided himself on being a self-made man. Although it would have taken a lot of moral fortitude to resist the temptation to get what he wanted through collusion, or by issuing ultimatums, with his religious training, or spiritual awareness, he could have achieved his goals easily without having to resort to these methods.

Although Henry may have tried not to show it, he had a strong tendency to be over-emotional. His moods depended on his feelings of the moment. When he was emotionally high, he was outgoing, but he was shaken by any unsettling experiences. Because of his emotional nature, he tended to lose his composure under stress. He became aggressive but only when he had to protect himself from abuse. He spent much time looking back to happier moments in his past and tended to hold onto memories of past injustices. He worried too much about childhood inadequacy fears that were still operating in his unconsciousness. He had many self-doubts when it came to expressing his creativity and felt a strong need to overcome obstacles that he perceived in his creative process. He had to learn how to stop perpetuating fears that blocked his creativity. Additionally, a hatred of restrictions and an undue love of change often prevented successful achievement. He tended to stymie himself, actually slowing down any real progress in life because he he had inner fears of commitment. He could have turned probabilities that he could have attained into such obstacles that they became too remote from his life for him actually to have realised them. Nevertheless he felt a need to create something of lasting value in order to feel a sense of purpose. He kept feeling that he should have been doing more in life than he actually was, but he tended to delay much of his productive output until later in life. He may have had to bear a heavy burden in terms of paying a debt to a child. Still, if he could have done this, it would have helped him to establish the sense of purpose that he was seeking. Yet again, no matter how much he would rather have been an observer of life, he kept falling into one situation after another where the full weight of responsibility was put on him. The more he sought pleasure, the more responsibility he found himself carrying. In great measure, this was to teach him what life was really about. Thus he forbad himself much that he really needed. As soon as he could have dealt with all these burdens, he would not only have overcome many of his obstacles but he could then, perhaps, have made an important contribution to mankind.

Relationships

<u>Others:</u> Henry's good diplomatic manner together with his desire for harmony in general for others resulted in kindly motives in humanitarian ways. On the other hand, he was turned off by people who lacked depth and perception. He respected others rights and, in turn, wanted them to respect his privacy. Being independent, he did not take advice well from others but he did listen and at some future date would have realised the truths that had been told to him. Thus his philosophical views on life tended to be different from those around him and it was important for him to learn that views could have been different without being valued as better or worse. His views would have been challenged by people with different ones, and those who envied his accomplishments may have harassed him. However, because he was secure in the righteousness of his own motivations, he feared no adversaries. Hence he could afford to advance himself through ruthless behaviour towards others. He could have been abrupt with them, often interrupting their thought patterns desiring that he himself only would be heard.

Henry may have felt that not only was he always making concessions to others, which made him feel inferior to them, but he was always having to conform for their convenience as well. Although making some concessions was a way to make contact with people, it may have caused him some anxiety. Because of these anxious feelings, he remained on the side-lines of society, where he felt more secure. However, he would surely have become lonely unless he had been willing to participate. In general, Henry was not easily convinced that people really liked him so he kept them at a distance. When he did allow people into his life, he tended to dominate them to compensate for his own insecurity.

On the other hand, Henry understood people's needs and was sensitive to their failings. He usually knew what they expected from him, despite difficulties, and he was willing to go along with them knowing that this investment of time would prove beneficial in the long run. People sought his professional services because he impressed his zeal for life on them, because they were impressed with his knowledge and because they usually sensed that they could tell him their problems and that he would then do what he could to help them find solutions. Thus, as a real instructor and inspirer of others, he could, even though he didn't know that he had such a talent. At the same time, he tended to dwell in the self-pride of trying to live a moralistic life. Possibly, a lack of reciprocity from others brought on depression, loneliness and an inability to realise that this was springing from within himself.

Henry was dependent on others for appreciation. This gave him a warm feeling of satisfaction. Wherever he went and whatever he did, he was trying to win the praise of those close to him, who could see the motives in his actions more clearly than he did. He hoped that he had helped people to know how to face the future with greater optimism and self-confidence. If they remembered him for his efforts, then he would have felt that all he had done had been worthwhile.

Friends: Henry would have been attracted towards home, brethren and friends. If necessary, he would have benefitted considerably from friends, relatives and charity, and vice-versa.

Henry tended to choose as friends only those people who were unlikely to make demands on him. He wanted friends who understood his feelings of inadequacy and his moods, which fluctuated quite a lot, varying from emotionally high to passively low. Because of this temperamental condition he was reassured by the company of people whom he could rely on when, occasionally, he needed their support. Thus, he capitalised on his friends when necessary but he was willing to reciprocate when they needed favours, even though he often assumed that people wanted his friendship only because he was willing to help them.

Family: Henry would have been happy with his parents and, generally, home matters would have been happy too. Providing for his children's needs would have stimulated him to extend himself. Probably, he was pre-occupied with giving his children every opportunity to reach their own goals and objectives according to their individual needs. He had high hopes that his children would have reached out to their destiny with the same enthusiasm that he had showed. However, he had had to be careful not to alienate them by telling them what to do with their lives.

Lover: Henry had a strong ability to love and enjoy sexual life, which tended to be more robust than delicate. His love was unemotional and detached in which friendship was preferred over emotional ties. Although sincere, stable and conventional in affection, there was also a delightful, intriguing and fascinating aspect as well. There was an easy slipping away from one attraction and the quick forming of another. Thus partings were likely for good reasons with pleasant replacements and reunions. Accordingly, he had little difficulty attracting lovers but his attention tended to wander once he'd achieved victory.

Serious love matters prospered slowly because there was a great deal of maturing to take place before an intimate relationship could flow smoothly. Fearing rejection, Henry wouldn't express his feelings for someone until he was sure that the feeling was mutual. Love was an important force in his life and may have proved the catalyst for his success.

Unless he was mentally and emotionally composed Henry should have avoided marrying early to compensate for any parental insufficiency. He needed a partner with wisdom and patience to cope with his competitiveness and to help him to become more objective and realistic in his goals. On the other hand, his partner would have had to depend on his resourcefulness to compensate for her failings. His partner should have realised how important it was for him that he had the opportunity to succeed or fail on his own terms. In addition, his partner must have been willing to share his emotional highs and lows. He may have married a foreigner, or have lived abroad after marriage, or may have gone into such partnership for business or professional reasons.

Career

Early: Henry's destiny lay in his own hands, in the hands of others and depended on circumstances. His fate depended on his early, unfavourable environment that contained repression and serious obstacles, so that there was little power to break away from early training. It was also affected by his innate self-control, organising power as well as, later on, his chastity. Great activity was likely as the result of a very eventful, changeful and hard life. Probably there had been a period during early childhood when he had been able to shine and, as a result, he kept trying to recreate the successes of this period during his adult life. His feelings of insecurity may have developed early on, when doing what his parents (guardians) expected meant curtailing his personal desires. He had needed the family structure as a foundation (which he never got) yet he tended to find a great deal of scattered reasons why those close to him had impeded his progress. He would have done well to understand that most of the over-reactions he experienced were due to earlier attitudes that were no longer applicable to his current situation. This pattern may have made it more difficult for him to establish an independent life. How independent he became depended on how far he was able to accept another person's authority over him. Resisting only impeded his progress and showed his incompetence. Although he realised that everyone must answer to someone else, he felt that the most crucial measure of success was whether or not he was living up to his potential. His future success depended on breaking with the past, which restrained him, and establishing what he owed himself. Self-analysis would have given him spiritual strength.

However, Henry mustn't have neglected the formal training he needed for greater polish and savoir-faire. It was essential that he improved his self-image, which he did by getting a formal education. This would have allowed him to compete successfully and helped him to cope with his personal relationships. He could have accomplished far more by finesse than by brute force. If he could have learnt the art of friendly persuasion he would have achieved the same results without wasting energy on unnecessary conflicts. In this way, education would have taught him how to deal with people and win their co-operation. Education had helped him to find a way to express his understanding, compassion and concern for less fortunate people. In addition, it would have enhanced his worth and enabled him to derive the greatest benefits from his creativity.

Henry dissipated his emotional energy thereby making it difficult for him to point his work, or career, in a single direction. He tried to break out of the emotional walls he kept erecting. Before he could hope to distinguish himself in his career he had to deal with his fear of competition. Also, he had to have been able to deal objectively with the problems of the real world and not allow abrasive situations to disturb him emotionally. He had to raise his credibility by learning how to blend imagination with creativity and use this to establish his position. In addition, he had to put a value on his services and demand a proper return for them.

Gaining recognition depended entirely on Henry's forcefulness in asserting himself despite hazards. He did have a driving ambition to make an impression on the world. When stimulated, he would have energetically accepted any challenge that would have shown his courage and ability. Having conquered his fears he would have found that he thoroughly enjoyed competition and the thrill of meeting problems head on, and when he succeeded, he would have glowed, literally. Success and prosperity was indicated. His responsibility would have been through work but there could well have been difficulties through workers. However, long-term results could well have been good using his patience, strength and endurance.

<u>Middle:</u> Henry had an immediate and practical responsibility coupled with a particular and rather uncompromising direction to his life-effort. He was capable of unique achievement through a development of unsuspected relations in life but was apt to waste his energies through his improper alignment with various situations. Nevertheless, he adapted his allegiances to lines along which he could have made his efforts count for the most. Success through foreign countries and people from abroad was indicated. Work-wise he could have been unusually efficient when he knew others were depending upon him for order and efficiency.

Fortunate in money matters, Henry displayed carefulness, some economy and a tendency to slow and patient accumulation. Because of his frugal nature, he probably would have accumulated a substantial nest-egg. There was gain/loss through several sources but he tended to squander money when he did spend it. His earning ability was tied to fulfilling the needs of the public. He understood the power associated with money and he also recognised the social responsibility that this entailed. His intuition/foresight could have helped him to make wise investments both for himself and in counselling others. He placed a high premium on his services because he knew he could get the results people wanted. His fascination with some people's financial advantages challenged him to charge as much as possible for the services he provided and he may have been tempted to take more than he gave, especially if he couldn't control his desires. Thus, when the price was right, he may not have denied himself whatever he could get, either in acquiring worldly goods or in satisfying physical desires.

On the other hand, Henry took great pride in being able to reach his objectives without having to resort to questionable practices. He would have enjoyed the friendship of his personal and professional associates, whom he could have depended on for support, if he needed it. As he reached each goal, he immediately set himself a new one, ever widening his sphere of influence among his colleagues and generally. He always had a goal because he never felt that he'd acquired all the comforts that life had to offer. He was sure of what he knew and he wasn't afraid to communicate that fact to his superiors. His ability to satisfy his employer's needs and objectives would have made him a valuable employee.

An important feature of Henry's life was getting involved in circumstances relating to other's needs, either publicly or privately. His deep concern for people prompted him to commit to satisfying their needs. This allowed him to make the most significant investment of his talents, which would have given him the most rewarding and enduring benefit. It was critical to his continuing development that he helped others to become more self-sufficient. In a sense, he owed that kind of effort to society because he was so intimately aware of what was needed. But he also had to cope with his own feeling of insufficiency and it would have taken him a considerable effort to satisfy the demands that others made of him, while still fulfilling his own needs. He may well have become overly pre-occupied with personal matters when he should have directed his attention to external affairs. However, until he felt secure, he would have focused primarily on his own interests but as he matured and realised that doing for others could be fascinating and rewarding, then he would have given them the attention they needed. If his efforts had been appreciated, it would have meant that he had developed worthwhile skills and had been making a valuable contribution. His self-doubts about his ability would have faded the more successful he became in meeting the challenge of competition.

Henry prudently provided, and easily received by return, support, help and charity, successfully to areas of deep study, to travel and to higher education.

Vocation: There would have been little ambition, or of rising to a lofty position in the world, for Henry. Some practical business ability would have made him suitable as a good servant or under-manager. Although perhaps too unstable to be a faithful servant of the conscientious and honourable type, he was possibly favoured for worldly success as his foresight could have been used for practical ends. For example, money may have been made by writing or from travelling. Communication in affairs to do with life outside the home such as business, politics and all public life would have attracted him. He could have found a satisfactory career in areas such as broadcasting, journalism, social service, public relations, education and even the ministry. Medicine, financial and investment counselling, insurance and retirement programs comprised some of the many careers that would have been suitable for him. Any of these careers and professions would have brought him into close contact with people who needed his sympathetic understanding. Knowing that he had been helpful could have proved enriching.

Late: Henry had a starkly realistic vision of the future and he took few chances that would have risked his security in his later years. He must have known that he couldn't have indulged himself during his productive years and then have expected others to have sustained him later. He became anxious to translate his ideas into tangible rewards so he didn't have to depend on them. He could have enjoyed a comfortable life if he had planned ahead for his future financial independence. Although he should have set up a plan to achieve his goals, he tended to dawdle.

Health and Appearance

<u>Appearance:</u> Henry was of middle stature and possibly short with a compact and well-proportioned body. His face was neat, clean-cut and trim with a smooth complexion. Deliberate in movement, he would have taken short steps when walking.

<u>Health:</u> Henry had good general health and an harmoniously working nervous system but petulance and worry, because of his refusal to accept necessity, could have affected his health. His sensitive nervous system, in which elation and depression alternated quickly, could have become stressed. Because of a lack of exercise coupled with indolence, he had a tendency to lock-up poisonous substances in his system, so that plain living was essential. Possibly he had trouble with his kidneys. There was a danger of accidents by burns and scalds, and by falls, chills and orthopaedic troubles. Physical overstrain was also risked.

- -

Reference: "Henry VI", Bertram Wolffe, Yale University Press, New Haven, U.S.A., 2001 Ed.

- -

EDWARD IV

"I am now threatened by a much higher, much more malicious, more unnatural and loathly treason, that at any time hath been compassed, purposed and conspired."

After his father had been killed at the Battle of Wakefield (1460) Edward inherited his claim to the throne. With the support of his cousin, Richard Neville, the Earl of Warwick ('The Kingmaker'), Edward IV became the first Yorkist King of England in 1461. Even at the age of nineteen he had remarkable military acumen (he was never defeated on the battlefield), a notable physique and was described as handsome and affable. The first half of his reign was marred by the violence associated with the Wars of the Roses during which Edward defeated the Lancastrians (and others including Warwick) in a succession of battles such as Towton, Barnet and Tewkesbury. After the death of Henry VI in 1471 his only remaining rival was Henry Tudor, who was living in exile. In 1475 he declared war on France but came to terms with its king (the wily Louis XI) at the Treaty of Picquigny.

Edward was a popular and very able king, who restored law and order in England and interestingly, successfully invested in several corporations within the city of London. At times, he showed bad judgement but, on the other hand, had an uncanny understanding of his most useful subjects, who remained unwaveringly loyal to him until his untimely death in 1483. Ultimately, despite his military and administrative genius, his dynasty survived him by little more than two years. He was one of the few males of his family to die of natural causes.

Edward was the third child and second son, but the first to survive to adulthood, of Richard, 3rd Duke of York and Cecily Neville. He was born on the 7th May 1442 NS, at 02:06 near Rouen, France (see Figure 24). His Epoch* (see Figure 23) occurred on the 17th July, 1441 NS, at 15:30. At Epoch, the planetary distribution is West showing that Edward's destiny depended on others and/or on prevailing circumstances. The Overall Shaping is a 'Bowl' with the Moon as its leading planet suggesting that Edward was set off against a complete hemisphere of experience, which he set out to explore. The Moon in the 4th House indicates that his mother's parental influence was paramount. Notice that Uranus is bi-semisquare to the Sun and to Chiron suggesting that help, advice and support from his partner could have proved valuable. Notice also that Mars (decanate ruler) is conjoint Saturn indicating a depressing control of impulsive tendencies and finally that Venus is conjoint Neptune in Virgo in the 10th House indicating a sensitive imagination with a strong idealism about his personal prestige, but a tendency to live too much in the clouds. The Sun in Cancer—Moon in Pisces sign polarity shows emotional harmony, psychic faculties and success in businesses connected with liquids. The Sun in the 8th—Moon in the 4th House polarity shows that he could have coped with his favourable but also frustrating, early conditioning for his personal development. In addition, his understanding and compassion for people would have

----

*Edward's Epoch on the 17th July occurs six days <u>before</u> his father departed on campaign for Pontoise. If we accept this astrological determination, then we could well conclude that Edward IV was legitimate.

Figure 23: Epoch Chart for King Edward IV of England.

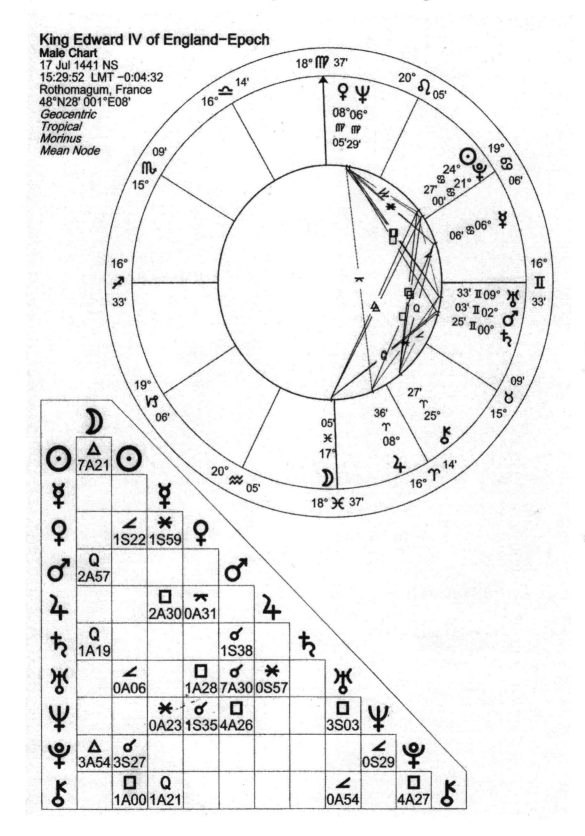

proved helpful to him both domestically and in his career. The Sun conjoint Pluto reveals a readiness to get rid of the old and begin the new, while the bi-semisquare to Venus and Uranus suggests an ability to stimulate others in their careers. The Moon quintile Saturn shows an apparently cool and cautious manner, whereas the trine to Pluto indicates that changeful, even violent happenings could have been turned to good account. Education would have helped him and being married would have allowed him to function at his best. The Morin Point in the 2nd Sagittarius decanate shows a generous, honourable character that inspired respect but that his fate was dualistic between fortune and misfortune. Basically, he would have tended to be impulsive and headstrong with a liability to go to extremes but this was controlled by Saturn's influence. Jupiter (ruler) shows his desire to enlarge his personal scope. His easy charm would have been overdone with trouble caused by too many love affairs and too much love of the easy. Speculation and risks would have attracted him but there was possible poor judgement here and in general that may have come from the poor working of his liver with his nervous system. He was both a husband and a friend to his wife, who probably wanted to grow and expand both mentally and spiritually.

The Epoch generates Edward's Ideal Birth chart (see Figure 24). Notice that, in the Epoch and Birth charts taken together, there are only four quintile aspects to support an interpretation of good intelligence. At birth, the planets lie mainly to the North indicating subjectivity. The Overall Shaping is a 'Bucket' with the Moon as the vertical, singleton handle. This latter enables a complete emotional placing of himself in any chosen reality, undisturbed by inner complications and so able to direct the whole of his energies to any given task of the moment, e.g. about the public and his career. Also there would have been a particular and uncompromising direction to

Figure 24: Birth Chart for King Edward IV of England.

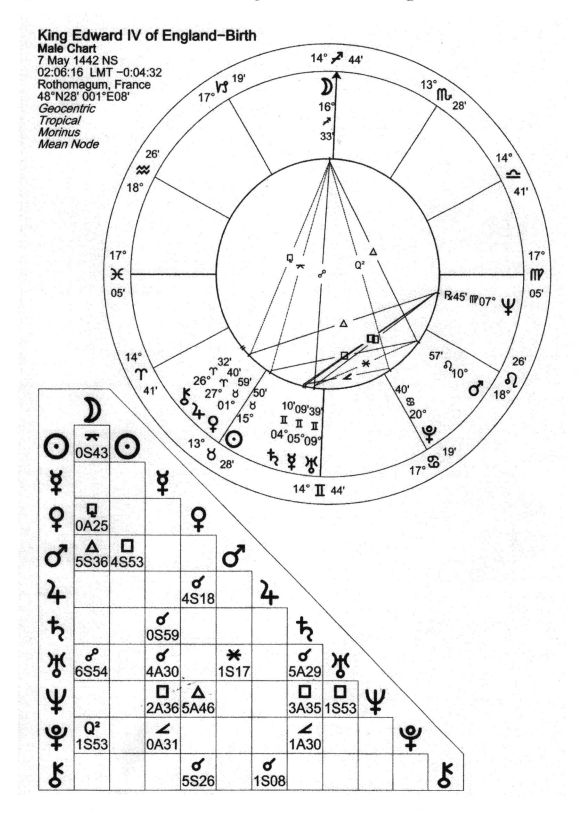

King Edward IV of England–Birth
Male Chart
7 May 1442 NS
02:06:16 LMT −0:04:32
Rothomagum, France
48°N28' 001°E08'
Geocentric
Tropical
Morinus
Mean Node

his life-effort. Notice that the Chiron/Jupiter conjunction is largely unaspected, save for a wide conjunction with Venus, suggesting that his cheerful and generous support, given assertively, probably was not well-integrated with the rest of his personality. Notice also that Mercury is conjoint Saturn in Gemini in the 4th House showing that his thoughts would have been seriously well-considered and deliberate. The Sun in Taurus—Moon in Sagittarius polarity indicates that he would have been inclined to go to extremes in all things; his personality being far too impulsive for his individuality so that promise often outran performance. The Sun in the 3rd—Moon in the 10th House polarity shows that although he preferred activity that brought him before the public, he was unsure whether he could withstand the abuses that he might have had to deal with. An understanding and experienced wife would have helped here. The Sun quincunx the Moon reveals his needs to be: (1) on guard against professional envy and (2) careful with whom he shared information. Also the Moon quincunx the Sun suggests that he should have been careful not to neglect his own importance. The Sun weakly square to Mars shows a tendency to overstrain through overdoing. The Morin Point in the 2nd Pisces decanate reveals a strongly artistic personality with an interest in the psychic and an impractical tendency to concentrate on visions of the future to the detriment of those of the present. He would have wished to become a channel through whom good forces could have flowed. The 2nd Pisces decanate shows economy, usefulness, the ability to resist vices as well as the ambition necessary to rise through merit and adaptability. Neptune (ruler) retrograde in Virgo in the 7th House suggests clairvoyance as well as peculiar conditions concerning marriage and partnership. His general idealism may have been weak due to overcritical coolness. Home conditions may have dominated his mind to an unhealthy degree (Neptune square Mercury, Saturn and Uranus all in the 4th House).

Character Portrait

General: Edward was a generous, honourable character, who inspired respect. His only drawback was a tendency to be self-righteous and priggish. His nature would have been forceful, compulsive and magnetic, conducing to results through sheer bigness of personality and belief in himself. As a result, his leadership would either have been obeyed or violently broken. He had been forced to become highly independent and so he had learnt to trust, and to depend upon, himself. He was ambitious without making an issue of it; he got what he wanted without making anyone angry. Any excess frittering of force and liveliness was controlled and although caution and patience were enlivened these restraining qualities may have depressed him. Emotionally, he was able to place himself completely in any chosen reality. Also, he was undisturbed by minor complications and so was able to direct the whole of his energies to any given task of the moment. Any special direction of energies was intense but he was also inclined to go to extremes in all things. In fact, his personality was far too impulsive for his individual nature. However, there was hope, optimism with a love of science and a tendency towards philosophy and religion to go along with a strongly artistic nature that was interested in the psychic, the mystical and the occult. All of these improved his personality that was generous, charitable and sympathetic. But his aspiration, being higher than his ability, meant that promise often outran performance.

Pleasurable activities often exerted a great attraction for him, particularly those involving travel or the outdoor life. Impressionable, fond of liberty, independence, sensation and novelty, he could also be reckless, extravagant and careless. Yet his manner often tended to be cool and cautious and so he seemed more limited than he really was. Duty, conscience and orderliness would have been important to him. He had a tendency to be timid through feeling somewhat inadequate.

Domesticated, good humoured and sociable his inclination towards economy and usefulness gave him persistency and the ability to avoid vices. He was inclined to get rid of the old and begin the new as well as towards beauty and ease but too irresponsibly and lazily.

Mentality: Edward's mind worked fluently, quickly and with versatility. His thoughts would have been well-considered, deliberate and with a serious outlook. Although he was harmonious emotionally, and receptive, his eccentric, quick-change mentality sought advancement in any quick and unconventional way. Genius was possible. He could be self-willed, self-insistent, disruptive, awkward, brusque and even revolutionary. He showed impulsive action, hasty speech and when provoked said a very great deal more than probably was thought or meant, while there may also have been a tendency to be very disputatious when annoyed.

Edward's orientation arose from division, i.e. from frustration and uncertainty. A state of nervous tension then existed, which could snap, causing much tragedy (especially when Saturn is involved, which it was). Relief may have been found in his attempt to let the energies free themselves by using his strong, galvanic force in engineering, science and invention, that pointed to results of an outstanding nature. Thus, serious, profound and prudent mental occupations were carried out at home.

Although Edward's idealism was weak generally through over-critical coolness, it was certainly strong regarding his personal prestige in life. He had an internal aspiration to become a channel through which good forces could flow. His subjective mind schemed in an involved way yet action came from intuition rather than from reason. There was a tendency for him to be impractical in that he would concentrate on visions of the future rather than on those of the present. His vivid imagination could have become gullible and confused so that his mind was not well directed. Touchiness induced could have led to escapism. For example, glamour and clouds of glory were to be expected rather than any real delusion but too much escapism could have led that way. Edward had mediumistic tendencies, much fancy and a desire to obtain knowledge here. Psychic sensitivity was present and some psychic factors were developable. Thus, clairvoyance was possible. He first perceived the future and then, as he was living it, realised that he would spend much time later reflecting over his past. He saw and knew that there was more to this world than what was immediately apparent. At the same time, he understood that he had to make his practical, realistic bargain with the reality of his presence in day-to-day living. He did well when he was able to synchronise his intuition with what was practical and realistic, filtering out, in the process, all that which was unimportant.

Finally, something was hidden from the outside world.

Lifestyle: Edward would have advocated a cause, or the furtherance of a mission, or an introspective concern over the purpose of existence. His interest in a cause would have been strong but there would have been somewhat less concern over end results, over self-preservation or over conservation of his resources. He was interested in what things meant and in what they were. He dipped deeply into life, scooped up experience and poured forth the gathered results with unremitting zeal. He had a strong desire to grow as a person as well as to increase his financial resources. Cheerful, generous support, help and charity, backed up by financial success, was applied assertively, but, this aspect of his character was not well-integrated with the rest of his personality. Perhaps it would have been useful if he, and others, could have realised this. Although support, help and charity was provided assertively to areas such as sport, creativity, children and enjoyment, somehow difficulty was involved. He was generous to a fault and should have learnt to be more conservative.

Relationships

<u>Others:</u> Edward was naturally argumentative and easily provoked by anyone who disagreed with him. His speech was too abrupt, lacking enough thought for others. Hence it was difficult for him to meet others half-way because he regarded any resistance as a threat. If he had tried to get as much as possible from others then his victory would have been bitter-sweet. Possibly, as a result, the promised strength of others was denied by their consequent unreliability in his life. Nevertheless Edward was eager to form relationships with persons with whom he could have expressed his ideas freely. He knew how to enlist their support for his plans because he never forced his ideas on them.

Edward always had something to give to his fellows. He did what he could have done for others because he felt that he owed it to them. He was an instructor and inspirer of others by stimulating them to capitalise on their own resources. He would have won their gratitude for his efforts. They would also have been attracted to him by his resourcefulness and dedication.

Through his tremendous sensitivity to other people's feelings, Edward became more compassionate as the years passed. He learnt to expect less from those who were less able to give, and, simultaneously, learnt how to build more within himself.

<u>Friends:</u> No interpretations relating to friends were found in the shortened, practical combination of indicators from Edward's epoch and birth charts.

<u>Family:</u> Edward showed to advantage in the family circle but his home and its conditions may have dominated his mind to an unhealthy extent. There was an uneasy expression of his affections with a

resulting lack of harmony. There may also have been stern conditions at home perhaps resulting from his responsibility for his mother.

Although Edward was happy with his parents, he may have decided that they didn't love him. He may well have been overly influenced by his parents' expectations but he was capable of making his own decisions.

<u>Lover:</u> Edward's affection was cool, undemonstrative and critical, but with a retiring, modest charm. This easy charm was strong and possibly overdone. He tended to allow his critical faculty and constant fuss about detail to interfere with his life's harmony. He was better with a partner because his desire for partnership was overdone along with a restless lack of ability to be happy alone.

Usually Edward reacted as a kind of secondary response to the behaviour of those he loved. While he could have gone through some disappointments in his intimate relationships, he would have been blessed with a tremendous opportunity for soul growth through sincere sacrifice. When he was married, he could well have paid a debt to his wife through sacrificial love.

Edward lived through a very spiritual experience of impersonal love in that area of his life where he consciously expected personal love. He would have had to draw on much strength from within himself because he would have experienced a good deal of loneliness. Much of the love that he expected to receive from others would, in actuality, have been the exact mirror of what he himself gave out. Thus, it was less the love from others that he felt, than how much they showed him the amount of love that he was giving out.

Edward's partnerships may not have been what they seemed. There were peculiar and unusual conditions about marriage and partnership. Possibly there was a hidden arrangement about these or that conditions were often kept hidden. Thus, although happiness was sometimes secret, sometimes there was also scandal. A disappointing childhood may have conditioned him to escape into marriage, which was hardly the best reason for such a demanding relationship. He might have chosen someone who was as insecure as himself, out of sentimental pity. There was a tendency that he wanted people to understand him and he would have been attracted to anyone who would have listened to his romantic fantasies. He dreamt of finding the right person to help him to exploit his creativity.

With Edward's understanding and compassion for people he probably would have attracted a partner who needed his support both personally and professionally to achieve an harmonious relationship. His partner was likely to have been spiritually minded, or artistic, but probably difficulties would have arisen through this and disillusion may well have followed. However, finding a partner would have allowed him to function at his best because he needed a mate to give him support and the confidence to fulfil his goals. In return, he was a willing listener when discussing problems; he was a friend as well as a partner. Basically, he needed a partner who would never have stopped growing and expanding both mentally and spiritually. Probably, he would have selected someone who was career minded or professionally trained. However, unless his partner was completely sympathetic with his career aims, it would have been better if he had delayed marriage until he had become established professionally. His mate should have understood that his career would have made many demands on his time. The promised strength of his partner was denied by her escapism. Although his partner's eccentricities would have exasperated him, he ought to have talked about career problems (such as extortion of the public) with her for she would have been honest and direct with him as well as being his most ardent supporter and helper towards success. However, he might have felt that his mate didn't give him the support he needed in achieving his goals. Overall, his partner may have expected more from him than was fair, but he thought of his contribution as an investment that would have enriched them both.

Career

<u>Early:</u> Edward's destiny was in the hands of others and/or dependent on prevailing conditions. Mostly hurtful and unexpected changes in his circumstances were likely. His fate was dualistic and usually divided into two extremes of fortune and misfortune. He was someone who always had something to bear. He must have realised that his destiny depended on the contribution that he was willing to make to fulfil it. Once motivated, he would have persisted through thick and thin to reach his goals and then grown and expanded in his career. He owed this to his job and to the people who depended on him. He couldn't have afforded to settle for less.

Edward's parents conditioned him to question his qualifications for success unless his plans had their approval. With an education he would have been ready to make a contribution that would have established his value and satisfied an important social need. He must have accepted competition if he had wanted to know the sweet taste of success. Possibly, he identified with his father in seeking the kind of success that would have fulfilled his expectations. Some disharmony in his nature, that would have been indicated by a cleavage in his life, relating either to his parents or to his early childhood, could have urged him to accomplishment. Later, he may have resented his parents' authority and their seemingly unfair values. Three questions to answer comprise: 1) How well did he succeed in overcoming his early environment? 2) And so, how well did he discover his own potential (by using his power for making choices)? 3) And then, how far did he go to make the best use of his own experiences?

Edward's childhood had been characterised by austerity and discipline, from which he learnt to accept or to take the consequences.

Because of his harmonious temperament, he could cope with frustration while establishing his position in the world. He had been compelled to make the best of the affairs in which he found himself, and his achievement must have centred on the increasing skill with which he learnt to express himself in simple either/or experience. Thus, he knew how to adapt to changes with favourable results but he may not have been as aggressive as he should have been. He often would have let matters wither away because he had failed to act decisively or perhaps because he felt that a better situation might have developed. Unless he had developed a plan for gaining the goals he wanted and was willing to persist in that effort, they wouldn't have materialised. He had ambition with the internal power necessary to rise through merit and adaptability. He may have had to exert himself in the beginning, but if he had persisted, it would have become almost effortless and even very enjoyable. His achievement must have been public in nature and have been rooted in his sympathy with the affairs of 'man' generally.

Edward was happy with life in the world and had a good, public, diplomatic manner. Self-analysis would have shown him that sacrificing selfish, personal desires would have motivated him to fulfil his destiny. He should have invested his creativity in helping others to create theirs. If his career had not allowed him to achieve financial independence through worthwhile service to society, then it may not have been a wise choice for him.

Middle: Edward had a tendency towards success but this inclined to be imagined rather than worked for. His schemes came to frustration because they were too impractical. He would surely have succeeded if his commitment to life had been based on providing the best service for those who needed it most. His wealth of ideas alone was not enough to guarantee success; he must also have been willing to work to promote them. He might have found difficulty in achieving success because he was too careless about the usual necessities of life in the world. Also there were secret reasons for his lack of success. Working with the public was his key but it involved many responsibilities. However, his superiors admired him for doing more than his share of the tasks. But there was an undermining of the power of control and of a completion of purpose.

Despite distractions, there remained a particular and uncompromising direction to Edward's life effort. He wanted very much to be in the public eye, and he knew how to take advantage of any situation to improve his public image. He adapted his allegiances to lines along which he could make his efforts count for the most. Although he preferred activity that brought him before the public, he was not sure that he could have withstood the abuses that he might have met in dealing with those in authority. He was easily unsettled by disharmony and he felt that his acceptance of abuse was a heavy price to pay. He also had to be alert to the possibility of professional envy from his fellow workers and to have had to be discriminating about the people with whom he shared information.

The demands of his career might have limited his freedom but through his accomplishments he would eventually have gained the public's respect and greater freedom. His desire to exploit his creativity might have been frustrated in the beginning but eventually he would have found the freedom to assert himself after he had learnt to be fully responsible for his actions. In all of this he shouldn't have neglected to consider how important he was to himself. He had an obligation to develop his ideas in whatever way would have helped him to achieve his goals. Serving others was fine, as long as he didn't sacrifice his own personal needs.

Vocation: It was important that Edward chose a career that gave him room for future growth and development. He was fitted for occupations involving athletics, horses, imaginative pursuits, higher cultivation of the mind or the church. Real Estate, financial investment, physical therapy or medicine comprised some of the possible outlets for his creativity. Ideally, he should have sought a career that brought him before the public so that the reaction he got would have been honest and objective. Thus, public relations, education and hotel management (i.e. clean, beautiful, harmonious and artistic pursuits) would have allowed him to use his talents in ways that would have given him the success he wanted. He could have been a diplomat, or contact man (and better with a partner) but results here may have been disappointing. Alternatively, success would have been reinforced in businesses connected with liquids.

Late: Edward knew that the financial security of his later years depended on using his resources as productively as possible.

Appearance and Health

Appearance: Edward was tall, slender and well-formed with a muscular physique. He tended to be a fleshy person with an oval face and a fresh, pale complexion. He had full, blue or hazel, eyes, brown or chestnut, and plentiful hair that inclined to baldness near the temples. He had a tendency to a double chin and possibly relatively short limbs.

Health: Knowing that success required determination and hard work he tended to overextend himself physically. His impulsive and headstrong tendencies gave him a liability to go to extremes and so exhaust both his mental and physical energy. When he was deficient in self-control, his excitability would have become increased opening the way for brain troubles and nervous disorders. There was some liability to hysteria. Although hopeful, optimistic and of good vitality, he lost energy through fits of overwork and by undertaking more than he could have accomplished. As a result, he would have become pugnacious and bad-tempered. By being more moderate he could have avoided exhaustion and anxiety from overwork.

His, at times, carelessness, woolly thinking and indiscretion (i.e. poor judgement) may have been caused by a lack of correct working between his liver and his nervous system.

Reference: 'Edward IV', Charles Ross, Book Club Associates, London, 1975.

EDWARD V

*"Alas, I would my uncle would let me have my life yet,
though I lose my kingdom."*

Edward V (at age 7 in the picture) was King of England for only two months until his deposition in June, 1483 (at age 12). His reign was dominated by the influence of his uncle, Richard, Duke of Gloucester, who succeeded him as Richard III. Along with his younger brother, Richard of Shrewsbury, Duke of York, Edward was one of 'The Two Princes in the Tower', both of whom disappeared after being sent (ostensibly for their own safety) to the Tower of London. Responsibility for their deaths is widely attributed to Richard III, and the disappearance of a boy claimant to the throne, probably arranged by his uncle, mirrors the presumed death of Arthur, Duke of Brittany, at the hands of his uncle, King John in 1203.

- -

Edward was the eldest son of King Edward IV and the third son of Queen Elizabeth Woodville (she had had two sons from a previous marriage). He was born on the 11th November, 1470 NS (see Figure 26) just before midnight at Westminster Abbey. His Epoch (see Figure 25) occurred on the 23rd February, 1470 NS, at 18:25. At Epoch the planetary distribution was general showing that his destiny was in his own hands, in the hands of others and also depended on the prevailing circumstances. The Overall Shaping was 'See-Saw' (there are 5 oppositions in the chart) indicating that Edward existed in a world of conflicts. This tended to make him indecisive but, at the

Figure 25: Epoch Chart for King Edward V of England.

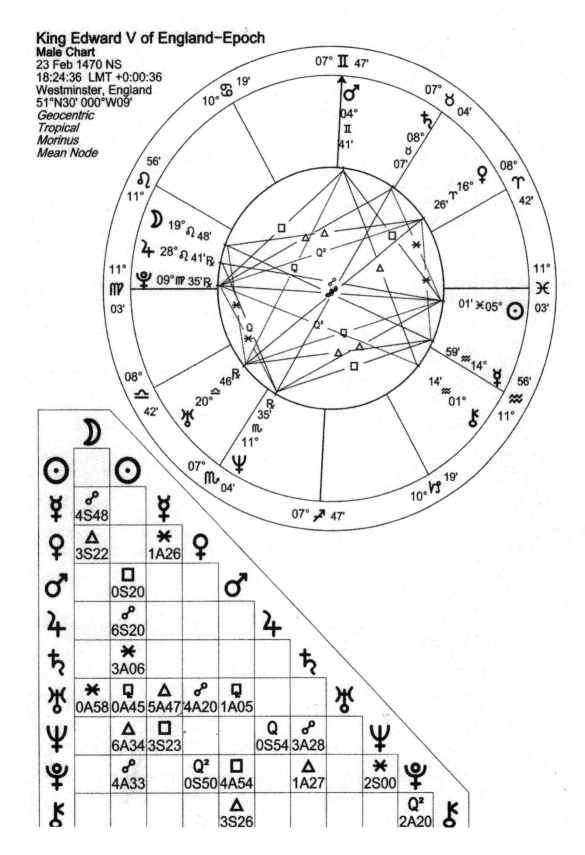

King Edward V of England–Epoch
Male Chart
23 Feb 1470 NS
18:24:36 LMT +0:00:36
Westminster, England
51°N30' 000°W09'
Geocentric
Tropical
Morinus
Mean Node

same time, his final choices would have been well-considered. There is a mutable T-square with Mars at the focus in Gemini in the 10th House and bi-square to the Sun and Pluto, revealing his attempts to by-pass, or to adjust to, difficulties but rarely without nervous stress. Uranus in Libra in the 2nd House is bi-sesquiquadrate to Mars and the Sun, increasing the strain on the principles of these latter two planets. This suggests change in his unusual financial affairs and that he would have been self-willed and brusque. However, both of these planets are subject to mediation: Mars from Chiron and the Sun from Saturn and possibly from Neptune. Notice further that retrograde Pluto, rising in Virgo, is bi-biquintile to Venus and to Chiron showing that his power of concentration was high and eventually that he may have decided to justify people's trust in him. The Sun in Pisces—Moon in Leo sign polarity shows a continual yearning for the unattainable, a love of the romantic, weird and mysterious and, possibly, an inability to maintain his position in life. The Sun in the 7th—Moon in the 12th House polarity indicates that he felt in complete command of his situation but was unsure of his ability when faced with a challenge. The Sun square Mars reveals that although much may have been achieved, his tendency was to overstrain through overdoing. The Moon sextile Uranus shows that his intuitions would have been strong, new friends would have been made often and that his moods were changeable. The Moon trine Venus indicates happiness in domestic conditions with an interest in the arts. The Morin Point in the 2nd Virgo decanate shows that he would have been quick-witted, adaptable and suitable for business affairs along with a love of study and books. Mercury (ruler) in Aquarius in the 6th House indicates scientific and humanitarian interests together with a desire to link up with like minds. Any excess worry might have resulted in intestinal trouble. Retrograde Jupiter rising in Leo suggests 1) that his feeling of nobility helped him to impress his zest for life on others, 2) that he could have been over idealistic, and 3) that he would have had a belief that he could have taught everybody how to live.

The Epoch generates Edward's Ideal Birth chart (see Figure 26). Notice that, altogether in both Epoch and Birth charts there are five quintile family aspects to support an interpretation of good intelligence. At birth the planets lie mainly to the North indicating subjectivity and a response to an immediate rather than to a future promise. The Overall Shaping of the chart is a 'Bucket' with retrograde Saturn as the somewhat clockwise handle planet to the Pluto—Moon opposition that makes up the bucket's rim. This shows that Edward would have had a gift for seeing to the bottom of problems by digging deep using analysis. However, notice that retrograde Saturn in Taurus in the 10th House is also the focus of a Grand Trine in Earth kite opposing a very broad Mercury—Sun conjunction in Scorpio in the 4th House, in which Mercury is the planet that is bi-sextile to Chiron and to Jupiter. All this suggests that, in part, he was serious about his professional affairs, that he was a specialist and that he was pre-occupied with money. Nevertheless he would have remained both cheerful and witty and that he was likely to have changed his course of action while working towards his goals. The Sun in Scorpio—Moon in Pisces sign polarity reveals a restless and anxious nature in which mediumship was easy, that he would have been mathematically inclined but with a tendency for deception and for ungratified ambition. The Sun in the 4th—Moon in the 8th House polarity shows that he would have cared deeply for those close to him, that he would have had a sense of social obligation and that his psychic ability would have served his career development well. The Sun quintile Chiron indicates that he would have looked forward to retirement whereas the Moon opposition to Pluto shows that he would have been subject to upsets and to forced new phases. The Moon trine Neptune reveals that much may have been given out through the reception of ideas and influences. The

Figure 26: Birth Chart for King Edward V of England.

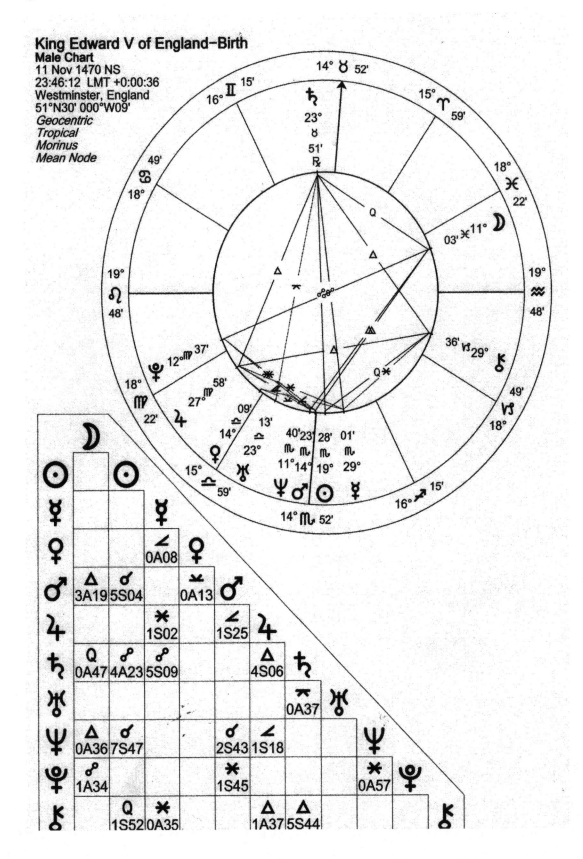

Moon trine to Mars indicates good strength physically and emotionally whereas the Moon quintile to Saturn suggests that his manner would have appeared cool and less talented than he was really. The Morin Point in the 2nd Leo decanate (the Sun, ruler and Jupiter, sub-ruler) shows an ambitious and power-seeking personality that would have burned for success but that he would also have had a liability to go to extremes, which would have made him demonstrative. He would have been generous but would have needed to exercise self-control until he was firmly established in his career. Education would have helped his career development also.

The following Character Portrait is probably not as relevant as those presented earlier but it does give us an idea of the kind of talented person he would have been, if he hadn't had his life so tragically cut short at the age of twelve:

Character Portrait

General: Edward had a studious personality devoted to books and reading with an interest in the arts (e.g. a love of beauty, poetry and music). He had well-coordinated hand and arm movement that would have been good for painting, design and craftsmanship. There was a tendency for him to be timid through a feeling of personal inadequacy. Quiet and retiring, he was inclined to respond to an immediate rather than a future promise. Fortunately, the tendency was also that these limitations were well-accepted, so that he became conditioned to what was lacking. Duty, conscience and orderliness as well as caution, patience and care were of importance and all were used in practical ways. His desire for more scope in life was expressed in quiet and unassuming ways. Wisdom and constructiveness grew and brought success in later life. His manner appeared cool, cautious and more limited than he really was.

But Edward had a restless and anxious nature. There was a tendency to wild extravagance of thought and deed coupled with an impulsive liability to go to extremes that, together, made him more demonstrative, active and, at times, even rebellious. Although his feelings could have been galvanic, causing upset, generally they were controlled, serious and steady. Similarly, impracticality, too much sensationalism and high passions were avoided. He showed some leadership and unusual ability. A keenness to get to the top in material ways plus an ability to work hard and push on in life were demonstrated but he was liable to suffer because he could have been unlucky, constantly thwarted and so revealed more promise than performance. Because his force was frittered away in constant changes of direction, his results tended to be ruined resulting in discredit.

On the other hand, Edward could be buoyant, honourable, righteous, proud, fond of power and distinction, fearless, open, faithful and determined, persistent, persevering and enduring. He was jovial, magnanimous, affectionate and benevolent with much warmth of heart, sympathy, compassion and charitable feelings. In fact, he may have benefitted himself from all these qualities in others. He showed enthusiasm for high patronage, display, dramatic sense and a desire to lead with a love of outward show, some ostentation, much social ambition, a sense of dignity, personal worth, self-importance and a considerable regard for appearances. These included a love of pleasure, of good living and of fine surroundings such as furniture, clothes, home, locality and scenery. Additionally he possessed a thirst for experience, great potential and a robust personality that made him adventurous, courageous and self-sufficient. Moreover, he was industrious with analytical skill that supported his scientific and technical interests. Yet behind all this he really was a homely and quiet individual!

Mentality: Quick wittedness, adaptability, a marked love of change and a certain argumentativeness were some of Edward's outstanding characteristics. Communication was expressed in day-to-day affairs of the secretarial, commercial and educational type as well as in affairs to do with domesticity, collecting and mental occupations carried out at home. He could be somewhat inarticulate so that sometimes he had difficulty in expressing what he knew. As a result, he could be self-willed, brusque with changeable moods coupled with a tenseness that was hard to relax. The tenseness derived from the difficulty of trying to blend his self-will with his self-control that also made him seem indecisive and vacillating. Additionally, his mind could have become restless, sceptical, excitable and acrimonious. However, his generally subjective, disciplined and deliberating mind together with his good mental outlook, charm of speech and an easy-working nervous system helped to counter these abrasive qualities. Edward was ingenious, fond of learning, sympathetic and candid, all of which went well with a cheerful, humorous and witty personality that brought success through its exercise. Alternatively, there was an intense and penetrating side to his mind that was strongly critical and mathematically inclined that turned to scientific interests and to those deemed to be for the good of humanity. He would have wanted to link with other minds similarly motivated.

Edward's obsession was Puritanism with a compelling need to achieve perfection. Edward's power of concentration was high with strong intuition. He had a gift for seeing to the bottom of problems by means of analytical thought processes. He was able to focus his unconscious so that he would have been a veritable dynamo in those specific areas to which he had devoted his attention. Unfortunately perhaps, he also had a desire for non-interference from outside sources because he drew enjoyment from working things out for himself. It was he who had to solve his own riddles and his knowing this made them worth solving. Basically, he strove to understand how things worked. His approach may well have seemed rather mechanical but it was the way through which he reached his clearest understandings.

Edward felt a strong sense of responsibility and had to account to himself for everything that he did. He reviewed the prestige and dignity he had attained in his past. Through this, he determined his current opinion of himself. As such, he was status conscious, particularly in his peer group but unusually he was also judging himself by comparison with past peer groups to see how he measured up to, or surpassed them. Unusually, Edward was attached to things, places and ideas that seemed to remind him of all he was accustomed to in his past. Habit patterns of these times repeated themselves time and again. He tended to be rather crystallised in this respect so that reason and logic may have eluded him if it meant deviation from his pre-programmed sense of duty to his self-image. The only way he could have been swayed is if it meant the possibility of improving his self-image in the future so long as nothing in his past was destroyed. However, he was capable of reversing any negative conclusions he had reached in his past. In their place he could have substituted all that was meaningful to him. And so he channelled much thought into re-evaluating all of his past burdens until he realised how much he had been accustomed to doing things the hard way. Unless he transcended his outdated approach to life he could have become a very negative thinker. Thus, he may have harboured anger at how difficult life seemed to be for him, while it appeared so much easier for others. Overall, he was trying to establish a sense of principle, which, previously, he had not found thoroughly, and truly did not have in his life in areas other than in his career, public image and sense of duty to society.

Edward was deeply concerned with seeing his life as some sensible formative structure, which had followed a more-or-less reasonable track from his beginnings to his present time. In this way, he felt a sense of having earned his security. Until certain, he may have experienced the fear that this safety and security could have been taken away from him. Thus, he had to work hard to make his inner sense of well-being a permanent part of him.

Edward's philosophical side was stimulated leading him to pose serious questions about faith and beliefs but this could have sapped his will-power. He was also much inclined to the occult and mystical giving a love of everything that was romantic, weird and mysterious. Although mediumship came easily to him so that much could have been given out through the reception of ideas and influences, his morality may have been weakened. Similarly, his intangibility could have resulted in some vagueness and muddles. Many of his ideas may not have been fulfilled. He could have become deceitful or, more likely, the object of treachery. As a result, he may have avoided the concrete, or tended towards escapism by resorting to day-dreaming, to foolishness and to craziness about "-isms".

Lifestyle: Edward tended to act at all times under a consideration of opposing views or through sensitiveness to contrasting and antagonistic possibilities. Thus, he existed in a world of conflicts. Although he was capable of unique achievement through a development of unsuspected relations during his life, he was also apt to waste his energies through his imperfect alignment with various situations around him. Consequently he appeared to be indecisive but his final choices would have been well-considered.

Edward applied himself seriously to the business of getting on in life that was often necessitated by pressing family responsibility. Work and energy were put into the day's activities. He dipped deeply into life and poured forth the gathered results of his experiences with unremitting zeal. He gave the impression that he was in complete command of his situation, but actually he was quite unsure of his ability to succeed when faced with a challenge. He attempted to by-pass, or adjust, to difficulties though rarely without nervous stress but any paradoxical results due to his own disruptiveness were expressed through harmonious ways. Continuously, he yearned for the unattainable or for something that seemed far beyond physical realisation. Yet he had a particular and rather uncompromising direction to his life effort. He did have an interest in a cause but without much concern for end-results and with no real desire to conserve either himself or his resources.

Edward was on a life-long quest to purify himself. During youth he was highly impulsive but after mid-life he would have become more introspective. Then, instead of wanting to impress himself on the world, he sought more to understand how much he was a product of the world he lived in. Although highly independent, he had to work at maintaining a reasonable sense of proportion so that he did not make things larger than they were. He was to continue expanding his self-awareness through his higher mind and he kept spreading himself out to increase the quantity of all that he thought was worthwhile but mainly he was attracted to all that gave the appearance of reward. Hence, he got to know a great deal about experiencing his outer self and he would have given this to others but neither had he to scatter his knowledge too thinly, nor to have appointed himself as one who sat in judgement of others. Basically, he was continuing a lesson in the evaluation of self-truth as personally he was forced to live his own philosophy. Accordingly, he tended to dwell in the self-pride of trying to live a moralistic life. He liked to believe himself noble by standing for some powerful idea, or principle, so that everything he did in life symbolised progress.

Edward was anxious to experience the future through his own individuality and so moved through life quickly, not liking to waste energy. He was highly competitive with himself in that he was idealistic and so uncomfortable settling for less in life than he believed he could have achieved. He wanted to be recognised for his progress. However, there was conflict because he wanted simultaneously to experience many activities at once, yet there was also a desire to start one thing at a time. Hence, enthusiastic for making new beginnings he tended to overextend himself and so leapt before he looked. And so he was a pioneer but not always on steady ground. As a result, one of Edward's weak spots was the hastiness with which he jumped to conclusions making him have to re-evaluate his judgements later. In all he did there was a powerful inner drive that motivated him. He was rarely content and extremely difficult to please for what he was seeking was usually beyond the grasp of those who were trying to help him. He would have spent much of his time transforming his personal concepts as he uncovered worldly reality. Although he was anxious to do this, his true progress always seemed to come from his own after-the-fact realisations.

Overall, Edward could have been more out-of-touch with his true nature than he knew. Unsurprisingly, his views of life tended to be different from those around him and it became important for him to accept that opinions could be different from his without being better or worse. As his inflated ego diminished, he would have been able to experience one of the more inspiring views of the world around him.

Relationships

<u>Others:</u> In Edward's active life experience, he showed a personal shyness with people. Yet he could impress his zest for life on others and so would have become an instructor and inspirer for them. He believed that he could teach everybody how to live. At the same time, he had a tendency to advance himself through ruthless behaviour towards others. Thus, he could be abrupt with others, often interrupting their thought patterns, desiring that only he himself was heard. He caused hurt to others in his attempt to get to the top in material ways. He was dignified when opposed, yet he despised his enemies. As a result, being independent, he did not take advice well

from others but he did listen and at some future date would have realised the truths that had been told to him.

Edward's talent allowed him to serve people's needs. He wanted people to turn to him when they were in need. However, it was painful not to know the answers to questions that people asked him. This should only have intensified his determination to be informed at all times. Within a short time, people came to respect his knowledge and his ability to understand their problems. The public gained confidence in him because he rarely made promises that he couldn't keep. People knew from experience that he always lived up to his contract. He understood what the people wanted because he had carefully evaluated which product or service was most needed and he tried to provide it. Soon, he did more for others than he did for himself. Though he was willing to make sacrifices to help others, he wouldn't have made concessions just to smooth the way in dealing with people. He had a sense of social obligation and the rewards that others derived from his efforts were significant and valuable. However, he tended to give others more credit than they deserved, underplaying his own abilities in order to avoid competition whenever he could. He also made more compromises than he should have because he assumed that others would have made similar concessions to him. This approach would have been ill-advised. By doing this he would have been suggesting that he was less competent than others and so had to give in to them. He should have helped only those who genuinely needed it. Eventually, he would have learnt how resourceful he was from the way people responded after they had benefitted from his efforts. It was commendable that his efforts would have made their security possible. He knew that they would happily have done favours for him in return.

It disturbed Edward when his efforts went unnoticed. However, with a little more understanding of how important he was to others, perhaps he would have gained more satisfaction after helping those who lacked his skills. In addition, he was curious about the motives of people who strove to acquire material possessions. People who showed off their assets really annoyed him. He was much more interested when they showed superior skills and explained how they used them for a useful purpose.

<u>Friends:</u> Edward often made new friends and he may well have benefitted from them. However, breaks in personal relationships occurred. He may not have been happy because he got from others the repercussion of his own awkwardness as a companion.

<u>Family:</u> Edward's parents' love may not have been as warm as he would have liked. Probably, his brothers and sisters sought him out when they needed advice. He cared deeply for those who were close to him and offering help when they needed it came naturally to him. He tended to be happy in domestic conditions and so was good for family and children. He was likely to have had many children and he may well have benefitted from them. However, he mustn't have devoted so much time to his career that he deprived his wife and children the pleasure of his attention and their mutual interests.

<u>Lover:</u> Generally Edward's feelings were controlled, serious and steady. He had strong physical desires but he didn't allow them to get in the way of achieving his goals. He was charming and lovable even though somewhat odd in expressing this. His unusualness was fascinating but could be somewhat unpleasant. Thus, breaks in personal relationships occurred, in which happiness proved elusive, and could have led to scandal and discredit. Probably he would have attracted a partner who was in constant need of attention and who expected him to yield to her demands. In fact, he did more for his partner than he did for himself and she may have tried to tell him that this was his obligation. If he had insisted that she establish her

credentials to him first, then he would have chosen the right one. However, his partner had to respect his need to be alone with his thoughts occasionally.

Edward's marriage should have given him comfort and contentment so that he could apply himself more completely to the demands of his career. However, marriage and other relationships were made difficult as his inner turmoil made him continually try to uproot and transform his needs and basic desires.

Career

Early: Edward had an ambitious and power-seeking personality that would have burned for success. Financial success was indicated as well as contentedness with his possessions. Business ability and mental alertness would have led to success in his career. Wealth was acquired through industry, thrift and by the adoption of practical, commonsense methods of business organisation. His destiny was in his own hands, in the hands of others and depended also on prevailing circumstances. His fate was governed by the social or political world through which distinction was sought. Possibly, he showed more promise than performance and so possessed a higher ambition than he could have sustained. Thus, there was ungratified ambition and difficulty in rising into his proper place.

Edward's indifference to achieving goals was not encouraging. He wasn't too impressed about acquiring status because of the restrictions that went with it. He felt that unless he enjoyed his career everything that he derived from it would have meant little. Similarly, all of his potential would have meant little unless he willingly invested his time and energy to develop it into a skill that the public would have paid for. However, it would have been easy for him to neglect this task in favour of more self-satisfying pursuits. He must have been allowed to think for himself, although he may have kept close ties with his parents. They provided reasonably good training so that he would have been able to achieve his objectives without too much strain. However, he may have been conditioned to repress his creativity, preferring to indulge his parents in their desires. As a result, he may have looked for a way to use his talent at home.

The fact that Edward underestimated his potential made it apparent that he needed an education or training. He came to know that to succeed he needed this and he should have got it as soon as possible. Education would have improved his ability to serve others, who could not have helped themselves, thus ensuring his own feeling of fulfilment. Rather than assume that he could not have done something, he needed the training that would have qualified him to succeed in it. His creativity merely needed to be developed so that he could gain skills and so be able to compare himself favourably with others. His good memory and store of knowledge would have served him well. His inner and outer worlds were well-coordinated, which would have helped him to derive satisfaction in his endeavours. Also, his highly developed psychic ability would have served him well as he sought to fulfil his potential. Important people would have recognised his abilities even he himself hadn't done so. Only self-discipline and hard work would have brought him the skills he needed to succeed. Once he had gained the credentials he needed, probably he would have become a specialist in some related area. He had to focus on gaining a foothold in his career. In his desire to develop he must have taken advantage of his basic resources. He was generous but should have exercised greater self-control just for self-preservation until he was firmly established in his career. Probably, he had grown up in austere circumstances. This increased his determination to acquire as many comforts as possible even if he had had to take a second job. He came to know how to take advantage of opportunities, and had no difficulty winning support from his superiors, because he always did more than was expected. Even a moderate amount of favourable feedback would have dispelled any anxieties he felt about his abilities. From that moment on there would have been little to impede his continuing progress.

<u>Middle:</u> One of Edward's goals should have been to attain a reasonably independent lifestyle and substantial monetary rewards for his efforts. Security would have been an important consideration when he chose a career. He was subject to upsets and to forced new phases. For example, there was frustration of plans when travel was arranged (except for duty journeys) and difficulties arose abroad with foreigners (unless elderly). Thus, he tended to be unfortunate in that he could find himself in a position that he couldn't maintain, which would have made him erratic and liable to varying moods. Change was also to be expected in financial ways such that money was earned unusually. Probably, Edward had hidden talents that he wished to exploit but he would have had problems trying to translate them into cash. He knew that money was necessary for achieving his goals. Hence, he was preoccupied with it and material possessions, largely because he considered them to be an extension of himself and tangible proof of his worth. Eventually, money would have become very important to him and few people could have matched his talent for acquiring it.

Edward adapted his allegiances to lines along which he could make his efforts count for the most. No easy path was available but eventual success was gained through plodding care and wise looking ahead. Caution and patience were used in practical ways. However, he hated to depend on anyone for support, so he tried to capitalise on his own ideas to make that unnecessary. Not wishing to appear incompetent, he often neglected to ask others for help in making decisions. As a result, he learnt the hard way from his mistakes. He was never satisfied with anything less than perfection in his endeavours and it bothered him greatly when he failed because he had expected too much from his efforts. He was serious about his professional affairs and he realised that circumstances would not always have fallen into place as he would have wanted. Therefore, he planned ahead to get what he wanted from his efforts. He was ambitious as his accomplishments proved. Essentially, he was a specialist and he prided himself on being the very best in his field. Thus, he was a professional whether or not he fell into that stereotyped classification. He would have brought much intuition, imagination and emotion to his professional activities and to any of his higher learning pursuits. Usually, he abided by the rules and was guided by firm standards in his dealings, so that the public could rely on his ethical behaviour in handling their affairs. He knew how painful it would have been to lose what he'd worked so hard to gain. He was determined to promote all his ideas to his own advantage. He was even willing to do without some of life's pleasures temporarily in order to guarantee his future security. He might often have changed his course of action in working towards his goals, which was fine, provided that he kept his primary objective in focus. It would have been ideal if that selfsame sacrifice had stimulated him to stand on his own.

After much soul-searching, Edward may have decided to do what he could to justify the people's trust in him. With his concern for the problems of society he could have applied his skills to help people to find solutions. If he had been willing to serve the interests of others he may have earned gratitude and sincere appreciation for his efforts. In this way he could have inspired others to follow his example. However, he had to make sure that he was not motivated solely by the desire for personal gain otherwise the process may have disintegrated and failed.

Edward was independent and adapted for business pursuits. He was suited to be an under-manger and would have succeeded as a worker associated with another, but he was apt to aim beyond this and fail. The career he would have chosen would have required public exposure. Probably, he would have earned his living by working with people. Public criticism would have seemed painful but he must have realised also that he would have won approval for his achievements. He had to weigh both factors before making up his mind—but probably he would have decided to go ahead. Counselling, medicine, research and financial consulting were some of the fields in which he could have succeeded, because he would have been stimulated to attain a high degree of proficiency and excellence. As he followed this course there would have been some intrusion on the time he wanted for personal indulgences but the satisfaction he got would have more than compensated for his loss of personal pleasures. He would have made a good governor, or magistrate, and would have shown considerable ability as an imaginative writer.

Late: Edward looked forward to the time when he could be free of daily harassment and of the effort of earning a living. The need to establish security for his later years would have helped him to maintain a plan of action and to see it realised. If he had used all his resources and talents, he would certainly have reached that goal. He would have gained the satisfaction and financial security that were so important for him for his later years through his achievements. Depending on how firmly he had established his roots, he would have been able to gain the security he wanted to indulge himself in the future.

Appearance and Health

Appearance: A tall, noble person with a full-sized head, a round face and a round forehead. He would have had a ruddy complexion, brown hair with a tendency to baldness and hazel eyes. Well-made, he would have had broad shoulders, large bones and muscles that would have turned into a moderately plump, square build in middle age. He had an upright walk.

<u>Health:</u> Edward had excellent strength both physically and emotionally with an enhanced vitality that would have been almost too intense. Generally, he had good health but not so well in some areas as might have been anticipated. Extremism in work and play would have led to overstrain. Similarly, though much may have been achieved, he overdid things thereby impairing his vitality, which would have made him pugnacious, bad tempered and liable to minor accidents. Moreover, any excess worry may well have led to intestinal trouble. Additionally, mental exhaustion could have resulted from too much concentration. Finally, escapism may have led to excessive use of alcohol or drugs. As his sleep tended to be over heavy, there was possible danger from poisons, gas and anaesthetics.

- -

Reference: "The Princes in the Tower", Alison Weir, Pimlico, Random House, London, U.K., 1997.

- -

<u>Comment:</u> There seems little doubt that Edward was his father's son but there are also traits here reminiscent of Henry VI, who was somewhat removed from him as a relative. Edward III was their first shared ancestor.

- -

RICHARD III

"Our principal intent and fervent desire is to see virtue and cleanness of living to be advanced, increased and multiplied."

Richard was King of England for two years, from 1483 until he died in battle (the last English king to do so) at Bosworth Field (the decisive battle of the Wars of the Roses) in 1485. He was the last king of the House of York and the last of the Plantagenet dynasty. When his brother, Edward IV, died in 1483, Richard was named Lord Protector of the realm for Edward's son and successor, the 12-year-old King Edward V. The young king and his younger brother Richard were lodged in the Tower of London. However, before the young king could be crowned, Edward IV's marriage to the boys' mother, Elizabeth Woodville, was declared invalid, making their children illegitimate and so ineligible for the throne. Richard claimed the throne and was crowned on 6th July. The two young princes disappeared and a number of accusations were made that the boys had been murdered by Richard.

There were two major rebellions against Richard. The first, in October, 1483, was led by Henry Stafford, a staunch ally of Edward IV and earlier, of Richard). The revolt collapsed and Stafford was executed. The second, in August, 1485, was headed by Henry Tudor and his uncle Jasper, in which Henry was victorious, at the battle of Bosworth Field. Henry became the first Tudor king of England.

- -

Richard, the fourth and youngest son of Richard Plantagenet, Duke of York, and of Cecily Neville, was born on the 11th October, 1452 NS, at 08:46, at Fotheringhay Castle, England (see Figure 28). His

Epoch (see Figure 27) occurred on the 25th January, 1452 NS, at 01:49. The planetary distribution in the Epoch chart lies mainly to the East indicating that his destiny was largely in his own hands. The overall shaping of the chart is a 'Bucket' with Chiron as the anticlockwise handle to the Pluto (ruler) opposition to the Jupiter-Sun-Venus conjunction as the rim. There is also an opposition from Uranus to Mercury close by. All this suggests that there was a particular and uncompromising direction to Richard's life-effort in which support, help and charity was provided cautiously to others but with some difficulty (due to difficult aspects to Chiron from Richard's personal planets, namely to Mercury, Venus and Mars). Saturn lies at the focus of a cardinal T-square being bi-square to Mercury and to Uranus. This implies that Richard intended to surmount his difficulties through reason. The Moon is bi-sextile to Venus and to Neptune showing that Richard wanted friends who understood his moods and inadequacies and that he was anxious about his future. Notice that the Sun—Venus conjunction opposition to Pluto (ruler) is mitigated by the trine to Neptune in Libra in the 11th House. Notice also that Mercury receives only difficult aspects.

Chiron, the 'Bucket's' handle, is at the focus of a Grand-Trine in air in which Chiron is bi-trine to Jupiter and to Saturn. This suggests an essentially intellectual attack when Richard tried to break-up, and then improve, the old order of things. The Sun in Aquarius—Moon in Scorpio sign polarity suggests a worldly and selfish person, who was very capable of playing upon others' natures. The Sun in the 3rd—Moon in the 1st House polarity indicates that he was intensely curious about everything and that he tried to be well-informed on many subjects. The Sun conjoint Venus shows that he expressed himself through his affections, while the opposition to Pluto reveals a

Figure 27: Epoch Chart King Richard III of England.

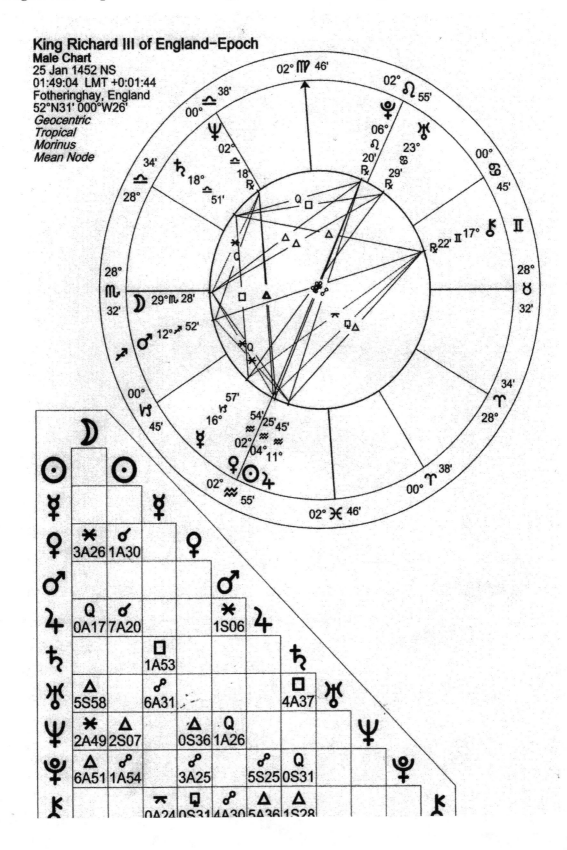

King Richard III of England-Epoch
Male Chart
25 Jan 1452 NS
01:49:04 LMT +0:01:44
Fotheringhay, England
52°N31' 000°W26'
Geocentric
Tropical
Morinus
Mean Node

tendency to advance himself by ruthless behaviour towards others. Education would have helped him to meet challenges. The Moon quintile to Jupiter suggests optimism in his nature as well as good health. The Moon's sextile to Neptune indicates that he gave out much through the reception of ideas and influences. The Morin Point lies in the 3rd Scorpio decanate suggesting the possibility of a criminal personality but also of a purposeful, hard worker. He could well have been sensitive giving a keen desire for attachment, which would have broken up a great deal of selfishness. Retrograde Pluto (ruler) in Leo in the 9th House suggests an obsession with megalomania and a compelling need to achieve fully creative self-expression. His concern would have been the overthrow of power for the purpose of transformation. Additionally, he would have been a rebel with a capacity to understand so much that he sought to explore all that he perceived in the world. We have already discussed the Moon (sub-ruler) but rising in Scorpio gives ambition, a fondness for fame and recognition and a desire for change. Mars rising in Sagittarius inclined Richard to feel invincible, generous and enhanced his rebelliousness.

His Epoch generates his Ideal Birth chart (see Figure 28). Notice that the number of quintile family aspects in both Epoch and Birth charts is nine that gives support to an interpretation of high intelligence. The planetary distribution of the Birth chart is South indicating that Richard was mainly objective. The overall shaping is 'Locomotive' and with retrograde Jupiter in Aquarius in the 4th House as the leading planet. This suggests that Richard strongly sensed that a task was to be achieved in the social and intellectual world around him, which gave him a self-driving power that was coupled with his own personal form of pioneering. Retrograde Jupiter is also the focal planet of a strong, fixed T-Cross (i.e. bi-square to Venus and to the Moon) showing that he was prepared to let difficulties in his relationships with women remain as they were and put up with them

Figure 28: Birth Chart for King Richard III of England.

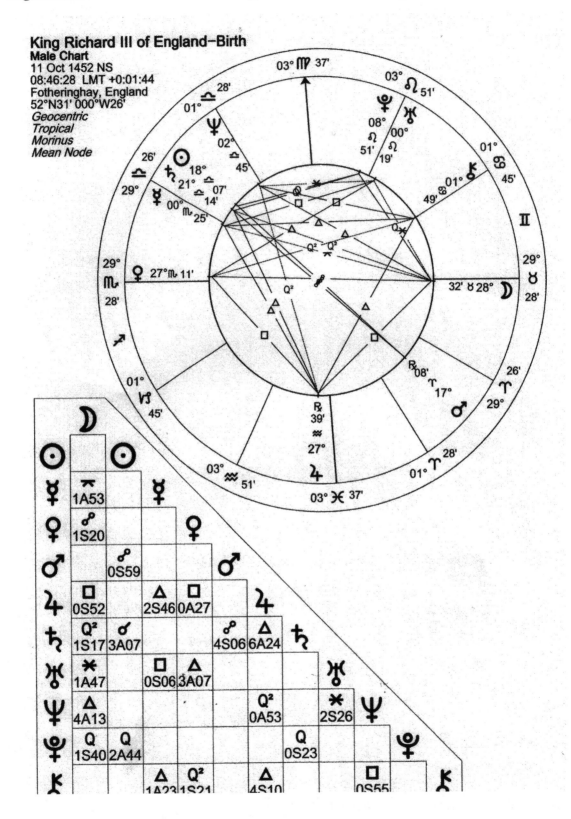

King Richard III of England–Birth
Male Chart
11 Oct 1452 NS
08:46:28 LMT +0:01:44
Fotheringhay, England
52°N31' 000°W26'
Geocentric
Tropical
Morinus
Mean Node

but the good mediation from Uranus would have prevented this from becoming too static. However, Uranus itself is almost exactly square to Mercury indicating strong mental action of the revolutionary type and of the too brusque kind that would have led to poor contact with others. Moreover, Jupiter is at the focus of a Grand-Trine in air/water that incorporates Chiron and Mercury. This suggests a good start in life leading to a thoughtful desire for improved harmony in his world. Yet, he would have wanted especially to be free to come and go, to travel and to circulate, among progressive others. Moreover, Uranus is also bi-sextile to the Moon and to Neptune, which suggests particularly keen and imaginative insight. Notice that the opposition of retrograde Mars in Aries in the 6th House to the Sun/Saturn conjunction has no mediation thereby suggesting unmitigated overstrain through overdoing.

The Sun in Libra—Moon in Taurus sign polarity suggests that he was overly receptive to his surroundings and conditions whereas the Sun in the 12th—Moon in 7th House polarity reveals that his many sacrifices for others would have distracted his attention and energy from his own personal interests thereby creating delays to his progress. The Sun conjoint Saturn in the 12th House implies limitation in his self-expression possibly through his father, a feeling of inadequacy in his background support and that he should have used his ability to serve others. The Moon opposition to Venus indicates an uneasy expression of affections and that he should have resisted the urge to marry the first likely prospect. The Moon square to Jupiter suggests extravagance, the quintile to Saturn implies some reserve of manner, the sextile to Uranus indicates strong intuition (as already said) and the quintile to Pluto shows acceptably changeful moods. The interpretations for the Morin Point in the 3rd Scorpio decanate, for Pluto (ruler) in Leo in the 9th House and for the Moon (sub-ruler) have been indicated in the Epoch and earlier (above) for the Moon at birth. Venus rising in Scorpio suggests seduction, jealousy, a liability to go to extremes and strong sex control. Venus square Jupiter indicates easy charm that was overdone and its trine to Uranus suggests an unusual but intriguing expression of love.

- -

Character Portrait

General: Richard's manner appeared to be cool and cautious so that he appeared to be more limited than he was really. Duty, conscience and orderliness carried out with persistence, perseverance and endurance were important. He was inclined to let matters remain as they were, put up with them and thereby would have become patiently conditioned to trying circumstances. If he had unwound periodically from the unsettling affairs of his daily routine, he would have become a better mate and parent. Also, he would have had more chance to enjoy his leisure time.

Richard's self-expression was through his affections, through beauty, art and gentle ways. Music, acting, dancing, psychism or, more practically, as love of the sea, were all compatible with his nature. There was optimism in his character and, when it suited him, he could be a regular, merry and generous sort of person, who was very fond of company. He was also fond of fame, public recognition, travel, sport and adventure.

On the other hand, there was limitation to Richard's self-expression, possibly through his father. He felt inadequate, or even effeminate, in areas such as secluded service, background support, escape or sacrifice. At his worst, he showed a criminal personality. Ambitious, tenacious, taciturn, harsh, egotistical and avaricious, foolhardy and even brutal, his nature was too positive, self-reliant, and assertive and so contained less admirable pride. Worldly and selfish, he was always liable to go to extremes. He was strong-willed and not easily turned aside. It was difficult for him to forgive, yet easy for him to be ungrateful. In short, he was someone, in many ways, who was rather to be avoided.

Mentality: In disposition, Richard was suspicious, contentious, rebellious, sensation-seeking and envious. He tried to break out from the emotional walls that he kept erecting. Thus, his higher mind became hampered by the insecurities of his emotional memories. He spent much time looking back to happier moments in his past life. This negative aspect also tended to make him hold onto memories of past injustices. At times, it became difficult for him to become detached from his thoughts because most of his awareness was purely of a personal nature. He was apt to be superficial in thought and to profess knowledge rather than to possess it. Mostly he tended to fall into the mental trap of over-expectancy.

In many respects, Richards had an aspiring, mainly objective and clear mind that was fond of new ideas. His cheerful, humorous and witty mentality gained success for him through its exercise. His moods were suddenly changeable but with an acceptable ability to throw off the static and start new receptive ways since he liked new phases in life. He was a rebel against restriction, seeing his world as a playground for him to exercise and grow in. He had a desire for change, a love of novelty and much curiosity. His obsession became megalomania with a compelling need to achieve fully creative self-expression. He satisfied this urge by using his skills in effective communication, e.g. in conversation, reading, writing, education and correspondence, all with deliberation, self-discipline and self-denial concerning mainly utilitarian things. Always, he wanted to get on with the next item on his list. Although he had intentions to surmount difficulties through reason, which he could have done using his good education, it might have proved difficult for him to revise his opinions on important issues when faced with new information. However, this refining process would have continued throughout his life, and he would have come to ask the questions that provided the right answers.

Not knowing something really bothered Richard. He was intensely curious about everything. He had a great urge to expand his knowledge, was eager to know as much as possible about a variety of subjects and so become as well-informed as possible. However, he became easily distracted and his attention tended to wander. Yet he worried about not knowing enough to qualify him when an opportunity was presented. But he needn't have done so because he quickly gained a working knowledge of any subject or situation, even when it was completely foreign to him.

Richard sought to explore all that he perceived in his world. He was constantly attracted to world thought so that much of his own personal thoughts became less to do with his own life than with the world that he was unconsciously exploring at any given moment. However, he distrusted the working of his unconscious unfortunately. Alternatively, he learnt that he was allowed to walk with his head in the clouds as long as his feet remained on the ground. Because he saw so much, he became very sure of his opinions and attitudes eventually, which could have caused him so much difficulty in relating to others. They were rooted in the day-to-day world of practical reality and so were unable to understand fully the sources of his opinions.

Richard was also anxious to experience the future. He was idealist and a pathfinder. He wanted to know all that traditional society had not yet explored. Restless, he was attracted to all the different paths that lay ahead of him, at the same time. As a result, he believed that he needed his freedom in order for his higher mind to work at its best. He didn't want to be tied down by any partnership but what he really needed was a mental rather than a physical freedom. Additionally, the thrust towards this freedom came from his early instinct to transcend mental and physical boundaries. Possibly he experienced claustrophobia as he tried at all costs to keep his life free of anything that symbolised entrapment.

Richard's task was to apply his past wisdom to future experience. To have done this he would have had to have done much travelling and meeting of new people from all walks of life through which he could have shared and expressed his knowledge. This was more of a giving process than a receiving one as he allowed much less into himself than he wanted to impart to others. Although he had the ability to understand so much, he would have had to learn how to focus himself on one thought, or one project, at a time, which surely he was capable of doing.

Richard showed psychic power and inventive quality but he was apt to be too receptive to his physical surroundings and conditions. Whether Richard was aware of it or not, he tended towards astral projection from one place to another and from one realm of consciousness to another, on an almost constant basis. He would have been learning how to cope with the full essence of thought streams, which were unbounded by individual possessiveness. He was one of few people who really knew that a person is not what he thinks he is. If used correctly and with proper training, he would have become an extremely spiritual person.

Highly imaginative and keenly intuitive much was given out through the reception of ideas and influences. His tendency to the intangible resulted in ideals, boundless views and strong visions, in which he saw only those that he himself had created. His love of the occult and of psychic phenomena would have become very marked, developing in him a vital (if not fanatical) interest in philosophy and religion. His ideas may have been implausible but his ability to apply them with discrimination was valuable indeed. However, he must have learnt how to withdraw occasionally for a quiet moment, to allow his imagination and inspiration to flow freely again.

<u>Lifestyle:</u> Richard had excellent prospects for getting everything he wanted out of life because, for the most part, he tended not to live in the past. He would have been interested in a cause but would have shown little concern over end-results, to conserve himself, or over his resources. He dipped deeply into life and poured forth the gathered results of his experiences with unremitting zeal. Support, help and charity was given wisely, cautiously and with long-term success. He also gave it assertively, quickly, yet thoughtfully and even harmoniously, but with difficulty. He strongly sensed a lack, or of a need, or of a problem to be solved, or of a task to be achieved, in the social and intellectual world around him. This gave him a self-driving individuality, an executive eccentricity that was not queerness, or unbalance, but rather was power. He showed a dynamic and exceptionally practical capability. Within this personal form of pioneering he was moved more by external factors in his environment than by aspects of his own character. Self-freedom was sought through revolutionary, free-for-all ways but softened by good communication, caution and by good imagination. He provided an essentially intellectual attack deriving from his sense of the social limitations imposed on human lives together with his appreciation of the need to do something about it, i.e. break up the old order of society so as to establish a new and better direction for human satisfaction (that is, a superficial rather than an actual attack). Yet he tried to create the future forcibly before any external force brought it about, but he would also have had to evaluate his past actions and to have taken full stock of himself:

Richard was primitive, subjective and actually could have lived for a long time oblivious to the world around him. He thought he knew what he wanted but a general overview of his life showed that he did not know enough about himself to understand his true inner desires, which involved a deep need to establish within himself the essence of self-esteem. He could have become so intent about discovering the truth of all that he did not understand about his past that he kept looking at himself too closely, thereby failing to separate the forest (wood) from the trees. He would have understood himself more after he had discovered the reason why his need to hold himself down was more important than his need to experience the outside world. Highly independent, he strove to be the ruler of his own life amidst a flood of external circumstances that dictated the direction of his energies. Thus, it was hard for him to direct his life in a single direction as he was more comfortable darting here and there within a changeable purpose. He liked to live a life of enthusiasm, and while he wanted to help everybody, he would have pushed away anyone who dampened his spirit. And, as he tried to order the world around him, he would have begun slowly to order himself. Still, his approach to life was unduly harsh and on all levels he would have done well to follow the advice of 'Desiderata': "Most of all—be gentle with yourself." When he had learned this, his general approach to others would have changed dramatically.

Richard's primary concern was the overthrow of power for the purpose of transformation. He questioned the validity of the 'establishment'. His desire for a world that he could have been proud to live in made him perfectly willing to tear apart all that had been built before him on foundations that he no longer saw as valid. He saw the world shift in values as a personal crusade, in which he could have played some intrinsic part. He questioned his identity by asking what he was doing to make the world more meaningful. He tried to project a source of secure strength built on honest foundations to a world that so sorely needed it. Hence, he felt an obligation to overcome all that had ever made mankind weak. And so, he spent most of his entire life with one goal in mind: to develop power first over himself and then, by example, over the false structures in society that needed more creative and honourable foundations. Although overly zealous at times, he could have become a great contributor to the evolution of mankind.

Relationships

<u>Others:</u> Richard was very fond of company and made his way in any kind of social situation because of his winning personality, which made everyone feel comfortable with him. He attracted people and encouraged them to be open and frank with him. When people spoke to him he listened attentively to find out what motivated them. Often he was rewarded with insights into their problems even if they hadn't said that anything was wrong. He became an instructor and inspirer of others and, generally, he would have had the support he needed from others, until he felt able to handle his own problems.

Conversely, Richard was generous in helping those who truly needed his assistance and he willingly shared his knowledge to help others to solve their problems but he expected them to appreciate his efforts. Those who had benefitted from his services would have remembered him and would have been grateful for his help.

Richard often felt that he owed people special favours though he couldn't offer sufficient justification for this indebtedness. Indulging people may have been a carryover from his early years when his parents made him feel that his greatest responsibility was to them. Perhaps he wanted their/others' approval or support because he was insecure about his abilities. Whatever the reason, he may have had to decide to work for himself, or he would never have got the chance to fulfil his own destiny. Without this development, there would have been many delays in getting established in his career so that he could then have realised his goals for the future. Many sacrifices for others would have taken his attention away from personal interests and would have denied him the energy he needed to develop his own creativity. Fortunately, this feeling of obligation to others would have faded eventually when he realised that people were taking advantage of him and that he had little to show for his efforts.

Richard tempered reason with consideration of people's feelings in an attempt to fulfil others' needs as well as his own. He was cautiously communicative and alert about support, help and charity provided for others' possessions. He may have felt that he was always making concessions to others, but he wasn't really sure that he could do without them. Making concessions was a way to make contact with people but it did make him feel inferior, which may have caused him some discomfort.

Richard could have been unusually cold where situations called for warmth because he had not yet learned fully how to trust other people's motives. He was highly conscious of desiring not to be used by others, and yet it was exactly this thought that made him keep inviting the very people into his life, who could have done that to him. He tended to resent others telling him how to do things and yet, without realising it, he wanted their advice. Hence, he was caught between the conflict of how much he should do for others and how much he should do for himself.

One consequence of all this was that Richard developed his tendency to advance himself through ruthless behaviour towards others. He sought fulfilment of his personal aims without regard for others' feelings. Great ability was shown in playing upon others' natures and so he tended to assume that he was the subject of any conversation that didn't include him. He developed a good understanding of people and their problems and it became rare when anyone deceived him successfully. Too often, he could have been extremely brusque, especially when he realised intuitively that someone was not telling him the truth or was being insincere. However, he needed to develop more sensitivity to others really. Too often, he saw them as competitors in the arena of his own growth, rather than as separate individuals with needs and feelings, which may have been as intense as his own.

Richard was seeking self-perfection through his deeds and, being overly critical of himself, he also expected too much of others. In some cases this resulted in a tendency to judge them. This could have been taken to an extreme in which his conscious mind saw no other human being as having the ability to live up to full expectations.

At the same time, Richard was dependent on others for appreciation. Also, although he may have tried not to show it, there was a strong tendency for him to be overly emotional. Wherever he went and whatever he did, he was trying to win the praise of those close to him, who could see the motives of his actions much more clearly than he did.

Friends: Richard was fortunate regarding friends and popularity. New friends were often made. He wanted friends who understood his needs and his feelings of inadequacy, but often he assumed that people wanted his friendship only because he was so willing to help them. However, he should have helped his friends when they needed it, probably because they had helped him earlier. Yet he mustn't have given into his friends' demands too often because they might have deterred him from his goals. A soft touch, he might have neglected his own needs to help friends or others.

Family: Originally, Richard benefitted through comfortable things of the home and family as well as having good relations with his parents. Hence, he had a good start for his personal sort of pioneering. The affairs of brothers and sisters would have mattered in his life and his family links were strong. His own home life tended to be harmonious because he showed practical ability in the domestic sphere but his uneasy expression of affections, at times, led to a lack of harmony in the home, also.

<u>Lover:</u> Richard's relationships with women, and with his mother, were not easy. His sense of lack, or of personal inadequacy, intensified his shyness/timidity and prevented an easy response to what could have brought happiness. A strong mothering urge was always in the background of his unconsciousness. In love relationships he should have avoided being the one who did all the giving. Somewhat later, troubles were caused by too many love affairs and too much love of the easy, the beautiful and the pleasant, at any price (but, as we have seen, he was tougher elsewhere). His affections and partnerships were subject to disclosures, upheavals and new starts with trouble and unpleasantness.

On the other hand, Richard was seductive with an easy charm that was strong but overdone. There were curious experiences for him to pass through regarding sex and sexually he was nearly always unfulfilled. He could have caused himself to experience periods of sexual frigidity sometimes resulting in complete impotence. This was due to his living-through-the-seeking-of-his-own-perfection in action. He had strong sexual control and would have ruled his partners. He had an unusual expression of love (or of artistic accomplishment) in any sort of partnership that would have been delightful, intriguing and fascinating. There was an easy slipping away from one attraction and the quick forming of another. Thus, partings were likely but for good reasons and with pleasant replacements or reunions. However, the sensitive side of his nature was also awake, giving him a keen desire for attachment and so breaking up a great deal of his selfishness. However, strong jealous and rather passionate tendencies were still evident.

There was gain through partnership and marriage but he had to resist the urge to marry the first likely prospect. His early training may have led him to believe that it was better to marry anyone than to remain single. With that attitude he could have ended up being single again. He sought a partner who shared his perception and deep concern for people. There had to be a spiritual bond in addition to the romantic alliance or he would have become increasingly uncomfortable in it. True understanding between himself and his wife were essential if their marriage was to last. His partner had had to have understood how important it was that they grew together. However, he could have been overly self-conscious, which would have been very difficult for marriage.

Career

<u>Early:</u> Richard's destiny had lain mainly in his own hands with a tendency towards a lucky journey through life. Generally, he would have been fairly fortunate for money, with sudden good fortune and success in foreign lands but there was a tendency for him to squander gains, to be extravagant and to trust to luck too easily. There would have been great activity within a very eventful and changeful life, during which he would have been uplifted in the public or social world.

It may have bothered Richard to work without recognition but he would have had to accept this situation until he was more confident about his abilities. In work areas, at this stage, he tended to underestimate the validity of his own output. He feared that he was destined to remain in obscurity but he would have risen above this with education. Because of his managing ability, he needed training in efficient self-management and in the best use of his talents. He may have avoided competition for fear of failing but as he matured he would have learned that competition was the key to his greatest accomplishments. He mustn't have allowed others to intimidate him because of his lack of training. In order to meet the challenge of competition successfully he had to have an education, which he enjoyed getting. He also came to know how to keep his lines of communication open to associates and competitors alike, which gave him an advantage over them. Even though it took a lot of hard work for him to succeed, it would have been easier if he had been well-informed and trained. With his progressive attitude, he would have achieved any goal that he had set his sights on with relative ease, provided he had spurned apathy and indolence.

Richard's early environment gave him the opportunity to develop and express his creativity. He used these advantages of his upbringing to become self-sufficient on his own merits. Probably there had been a period during childhood when he had been able to shine and so he kept trying to recreate symbols of this period during his adult life. He had needed the family structure as a foundation, yet he had tended to find a great number of scattered reasons why those close to him impeded his progress. He would have done well to understand that most of the over-reactions he had experienced were due to early life attitudes that were no longer applicable to his current situation.

Richard mustn't have avoided the responsibility for making his own life. He would have had to stand on his own before he could hope to achieve any accomplishments. If he had waited for his parents' approval he would never have established his own goals. He admired people who could themselves get what they wanted. Provided that his criminal tendencies could have been resisted, honest success could have been achieved by means of a thrusting, purposeful nature and a capacity for hard work. He couldn't have afforded to turn down chances for advancement.

On the other hand, he didn't have to need anyone's approval to rise to prominence, if he was willing to use his talents to benefit the public. Accordingly, the practical was over-valued with a tendency to meet hardships. Although life was rigorous or hard, lessons of duty and self-control were learnt. He didn't really fear occasional reverses and set-backs because he believed in himself. His attitude encouraged others to seek his assistance in developing the same positive outlook in their own lives.

Richard's great imagination was an asset that would have enabled him to derive ways to use his resources. This would have benefitted the general public in more ways than he could have realised. His depth of understanding and his compassion for less fortunate individuals could have proved the foundation on which to build enriching life experiences.

Middle: Richard had to have found ways to translate his imaginative ideas into worthwhile activity. Although he never lost sight of the future and of the goals that he knew how to plan for and achieve, still he tended to dawdle. His winning ways brought him support and enthusiasm for his proposals. However, he was cautious about revealing all his plans for fear of losing his advantage over others. Additionally, he may have had to maintain a low profile in his achievements. Moreover, he adapted his allegiances to lines along which he could make his efforts count for the most. Although he was capable of "drawing a bow at a venture with telling effect", his constructiveness could only have forced to a patient working out of what was begun but not with ease. His results had to have been battled for. The narrowness engendered produced selfishness and egocentricity. Hardship was endured and sternness given. He could have achieved much more once he had measured himself against himself rather than against other people, or against outside forces beyond his control. Sometimes, in dissipating his emotional energy, he made it difficult for himself to point his work, or career, in a single direction. In addition, his career may have caused some problems in personal relationships if his partner had resented the attention he devoted to it.

Richard could have fulfilled his own needs by using his ability to serve others. In fact, his destiny would have been truly satisfied only if he had exerted pressure in the right places to help him to improve social conditions. Observing, or learning, about human suffering affected him deeply but he could have done something about it. However, he wanted to know that his efforts would have helped to improve the quality of life for as many people in society as possible. Making a contribution that improved this would have allowed him to reach the limit of his potential.

Vocation: Some careers that would have been suitable for Richard include: public relations, sales, marriage counselling, law, social service, vocational guidance, or any other that would have brought him into close contact with the public. His practical nature would have been useful for executive, business, and firm, steady and hard-working affairs with suitability for prominence and responsibility. He would have been likely to gain money, property and dignity. His active imagination and creativity would have been useful for journalism, reporting, writing and education as appropriate media for self-expression. As a good soldier or sailor he would have delighted in military affairs and railway enterprises, etc. Additionally, he would have inclined to chemistry, surgery or practical research (as distinct from theory). However, perhaps most interestingly, he would have been able to undertake huge building schemes.

Late: If Richard had hoped to achieve security later on, he must have planned his goals for the future early. He was deeply concerned about this and whether he would have had sufficient resources to maintain himself. He should have started to think about becoming independent so that he could have reached the goals he had chosen.

Appearance and Health

Appearance: Richard was above average height with a tendency to become well-built and stout later with somewhat bulky features. At his worst, his nose would have appeared deformed or with a broken appearance. However, at his best, he would have been well-proportioned with a good complexion. Facial features would have included dark brown or grey eyes with prominent brows, an aquiline or Jewish type of nose and profile, as well as dark and thick brown hair.

Health: Richard had good health in general and would have been a good sleeper. Though much may have been achieved, his tendency was to overstrain both physically and mentally thereby impairing his vitality and so making him pugnacious and bad-tempered. As a result, he was liable to minor accidents of the burns, scalds and falling type. Support, help and charity would have been given thoughtfully but with some nervous tension. Worry may have led to intestinal trouble. There was the possibility of his being liable to unusual diseases and there may have been some danger met while abroad.

-- --

Reference: "Richard III", Charles Ross, Methuen, London, U.K., 1981.

-- --

APPENDIX

The Line of Plantagenet Male Descent

Now that we have interpreted all the natal charts of the Plantagenet kings and have produced their individual character portraits, we can now look at them astrologically as a group. Previously, this group has been called the "Plantagenet Dynasty". To bolster the group just a little we have included the Epoch (see Figure 29) and the Birth (see Figure 30) charts of Edward, the Black Prince, the eldest son of Edward III and the father of Richard II. The Black Prince's charts are interesting because, together, they show nine quintile family aspects to support an interpretation of high intelligence, as we have just seen in the charts of Richard III.

The common feature of all-male family groups like this is that each member contains an identical Y-chromosome as part of his genetic make-up. Consequently, we should like to see, and we shall, if there are any astrological, hereditary traits that are common to all, or several, of the members of the Plantagenet group. For any person's astrological chart there are three main indicators for interpretation, i.e. the sign and House positions of the Sun, of the Moon and of the sign position of the Morin Point. First, let us take a look at these. We have thirty charts altogether, twelve zodiacal signs and twelve Houses of Heaven. As a result of listing all the positions of the Sun, and of the Moon separately, by sign and by House, as well as all the sign positions of the Morin Point, we find that the Sun lies mostly in the 11th House (6X)[1], that the Moon lies in Taurus mostly (6X) and also mainly in the 10th House (6X) as the only distributions of any significance.

We also see that the overall shapings of the charts are predominantly those containing planetary oppositions; namely 'See-

Figure 29: Epoch Chart for Edward, the Black Prince.

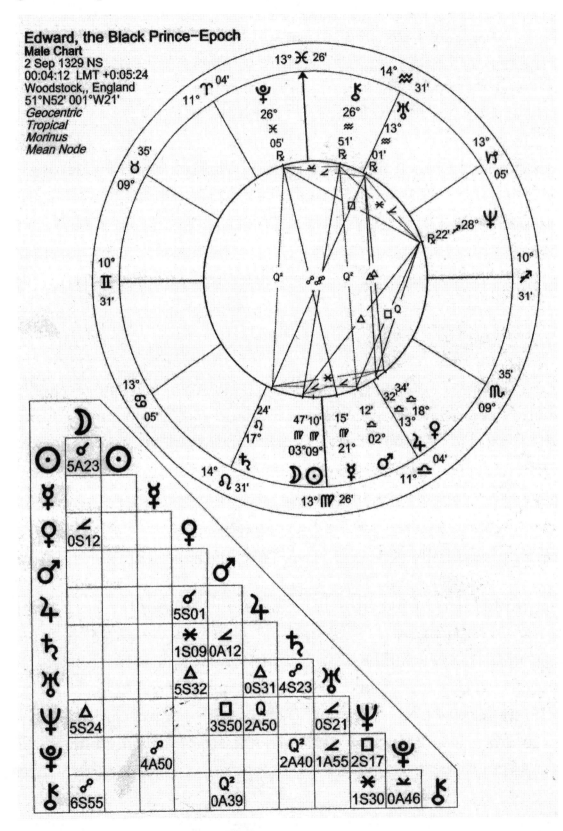

Figure 30: Birth Chart for Edward, the Black Prince.

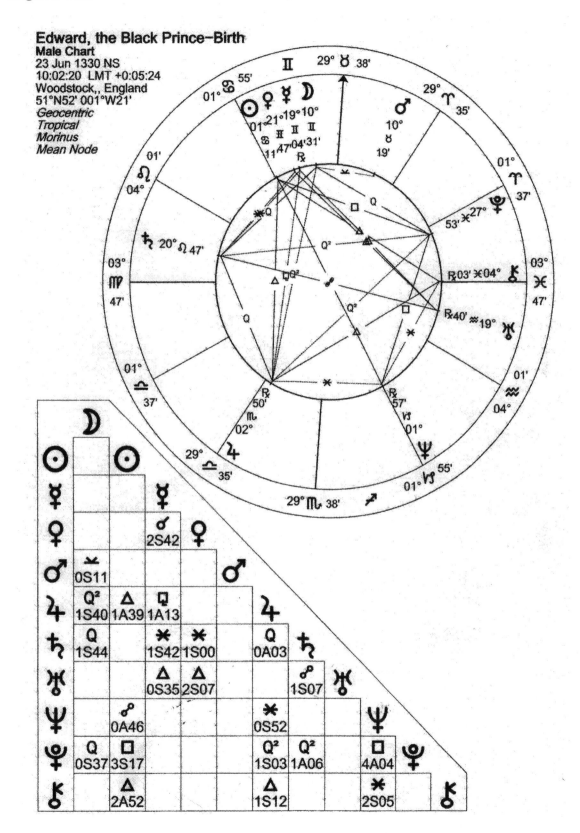

Edward, the Black Prince–Birth
Male Chart
23 Jun 1330 NS
10:02:20 LMT +0:05:24
Woodstock,, England
51°N52' 001°W21'
Geocentric
Tropical
Morinus
Mean Node

Saw' (9X) and 'Bucket' (9X). All these observations, however, are only indicative rather than definitive, because a sample size of thirty, in this case, is too small.

If, however, we now consider all of the planets[2] (330) and plot their occupancy as a polar graph (see the graph) in thirty-six equal Morinus sectors around the circle of the ecliptic (setting the Morin Point as the origin every time for each of the thirty charts), then the sample size is sufficiently large enough statistically. The expected number of planets occupying each sector is 9.167 (330 divided by 36) and we expect that the number of planets occupying any half of the graph will be 165. We find that there are 174 planets in the top half and 156 in the bottom one. This suggests that the Plantagenet kings were slightly more objective than subjective. Similarly there are 174 planets in the left half of the graph compared with 156 of them in the right half. This suggests that their destiny was slightly more in their own hands rather than depending on external factors. If we now look at the graph more particularly we see that the top left quarter contains a rather large bump protruding beyond the circle of expected values (corresponding roughly to the 11th and 10th Houses) that supports the combined findings for the House positions of the Sun and Moon, mentioned earlier. This suggests that the kings showed general interest in friends, objectives and in their career. There is also a small protruding bump corresponding roughly with the 1st House indicating personal concerns. This top left quarter also shows a considerable deficiency of planets around the 12th House area showing a probable lack of uncertainty as well as of background support. The opposite, bottom right, quarter simply shows deficiency throughout, corresponding to the 5th and 6th Houses roughly, suggesting some lack of creativity and of health concerns. All this seems to fit quite well with what we know of the Plantagenet group.

The Polar Graph:

Having set the Morin Point as the Origin in all of the Epoch and Birth Charts (30) of the Plantagenet Kings Group (15), the Occupancy of all the Planets (330) was determined in equal (10⁰) Morinus Sectors (1—> 36) around the Circle of the Ecliptic, and then plotted:

THE MORIN POINT AS THE ORIGIN OF SECTOR POSITIONS 1-36 AROUND THE ECLIPTIC, THEIR OCCUPANCY BY ALL THE PLANETS [330] IN THE EPOCH AND BIRTH CHARTS [30] OF THE PLANTAGENET KINGS GROUP.

-------- EXPECTED VALUE [9.167]

SCALE: 1cm ≡ 2 PLANETS IN A SECTOR. $\sum x^2 = 27.6$ P ≥ 87%
174 above; 156 below
174 to the left, 156 to the right.

Overall, for the graph, $\sum\chi^2$ is 27.6 with a P value of 87% providing us with some confidence that our results are valid, and that our initial birth data is perhaps not quite as unreliable as might have been expected.

We have also looked at all of the planets (excepting Chiron) by means of harmonic analysis using the 'Jigsaw 2' computer program, which can show number harmonics that are important for this family group. We found that, of the first twenty harmonics, the 2nd harmonic (corresponding to the opposition aspect between planets) at 26^0 Taurus, has a χ^2 value of 14.3 (c.f. that for the 1st harmonic is 5.1). This indicates that the kings existed in a world of conflict. Also the complete (i.e. no vacant points) 11th harmonic (the undecile family of aspects) at 27^0 Aries, shows a χ^2 value of 11.7 indicating gentility. Further, the complete 7th harmonic (the septile family of aspects) at 16^0 Taurus, shows a χ^2 value of 10.0 suggesting transformation. Here also, these results could well fit with what we know generally about the Plantagenet group.

- -

[1] The Sun and Moon House position results, in combination with the structure of the Morinus House System, suggests that we should compare the preceding graph obtained by plotting Morinus House sectors with those obtained by setting the East Point as the origin of each of the charts and using 1) equal sectors of right ascension around the circle of the Equator, and, for completeness, using 2) equal sectors of azimuth around the circle of the Rational Horizon. We should then be able to see which graph is the most appropriate for this pilot study.

[2] Mercury and Venus always occur within 3 or 5 sectors of the Sun's sector, respectively. For now, we have ignored this complication. Additionally, there is no control group for the Plantagenet kings group.

- -